D0193334

More Praise for *War and the American Presidency*

"[A] humane and powerful book."
—James Chace, *New York Review of Books*

"Arthur M. Schlesinger, Jr., the dean of American historians and an active Democrat, published his first book in 1939. This slim, gracefully written new volume demonstrates that he is still going strong. . . . Instead of polemicizing, he provides valuable historical information and analyses that he hopes will raise the discussion to a higher level."
—William L. O'Neil, *New Leader*

"This elegant and learned little book . . . offers a luminous and provocative guide for the perplexed in times of war."
—Josef Joffe, *Washington Post Book World*

"Provocative . . . a typically erudite history and an impassioned argument against President Bush's concept of preventive war. . . . Readers across the political spectrum will find much to admire in Schlesinger's scholarship and writing style." —Teresa K. Weaver, *Atlanta Journal-Constitution*

"Schlesinger draws on familiar historical material to provide entry points for exploring the relationship between Iraq and our national past. . . . To these lights he exposes the current occupant of 'The Imperial Presidency.' " —*New York Times*

"A vigorous lesson about the peril of keeping an arrogant moralist in the White House." —Michael Kazin, *The Nation*

"If you want a cogent, highly learned and historically erudite presentation of the case against President George W. Bush, this short but meaty essay by Arthur Schlesinger, Jr., is just what the (non-spin) doctors ordered."
—Joseph Losos, *St. Louis Post-Dispatch*

"A thoughtful book by a man who speaks not only with weighty scholarly authority, but also with the heft of one who has actually served in government. *War and the American Presidency* is a worthy capstone to a long and distinguished career." —Ross K. Baker, *Trenton Times*

"Scholars of the U.S. presidency and U.S. foreign policy owe Schlesinger a debt for his timely volume on presidential power and the Bush presidency. Schlesinger, incisive and eloquent as always . . . places the Bush doctrine and the war against Iraq in historical context, tracing the evolution of presidential power and U.S. national security doctrine from the earliest presidencies to the Bush presidency."
—W. W. Newmann, *Choice*

"Americans debating the war in Iraq might welcome a little historical perspective provided by one of the nation's great historians. Arthur Schlesinger, Jr., eagerly obliges with good food for thought on how war has affected the presidency over the last 200 years."
—J. Michael Parker, *San Antonio Express-News*

"The dean of American historians is angry. . . . [A] series of spry meditations on the presidency, the subject to which [Schlesinger] has devoted more than six decades of close attention. As with all previous works by Schlesinger, it is deeply informed and moves effortlessly between different epochs. . . . Signals that Schlesinger has reached a boiling point that even McCarthyism and Vietnam failed to bring him to. This impassioned jeremiad should be read by anyone wondering how American history fits with the perplexing problems of the present and a world that seems to grow more hateful by the day." —Ted Widmer, *Chicago Tribune*

BOOKS BY ARTHUR M. SCHLESINGER, JR.

Orestes A. Brownson: A Pilgrim's Progress (1939)

The Age of Jackson (1945)

The Vital Center (1949)

The General and the President, with Richard H. Rovere (1951)

The Age of Roosevelt: I, The Crisis of the Old Order (1957)

The Age of Roosevelt: II, The Coming of the New Deal (1958)

The Age of Roosevelt: III, The Politics of Upheaval (1960)

Kennedy or Nixon: Does It Make Any Difference? (1960)

The Politics of Hope (1963)

A Thousand Days: John F. Kennedy in the White House (1965)

The Bitter Heritage: Vietnam and American Democracy (1966)

The Crisis of Confidence (1969)

The Imperial Presidency (1973)

Robert Kennedy and His Times (1978)

The Cycles of American History (1986)

The Disuniting of America (1991)

A Life in the Twentieth Century: I, Innocent Beginnings (2000)

Schlesinger, Arthur M.
War and the American
presidency /
c2004.
33305229143767
la   02/12/14

WAR AND THE AMERICAN PRESIDENCY

ARTHUR M. SCHLESINGER, JR.

W. W. NORTON & COMPANY

NEW YORK   LONDON

Copyright © 2005, 2004 by Arthur M. Schlesinger, Jr.

All rights reserved
Printed in the United States of America
First published as a Norton paperback 2005

Portions of this book originally appeared in *Understanding Unilateralism in American Foreign Relations*, copyright © 2000 Chatham House; "Back to the Womb?" copyright © 1995 *Foreign Affairs*; "Eyeless in Iraq," copyright © 2003 *New York Review of Books, Inc.*; *The Imperial Presidency*, copyright © 1998 Houghton Mifflin; *A Badly Flawed Election*, copyright © 2002 The New Press; "Has Democracy a Future?" copyright © *Foreign Affairs* 1998; "Holy War," copyright 2005 *Playboy*; and *The Bitter Heritage*, copyright © 1966, and renewed 1994 by Arthur M. Schlesinger, Jr. Reprinted by permission of Houghton Mifflin Company. All rights reserved. And to the extent they are reprinted here, they are reprinted with permission.

For information about permission to reproduce selections from this book, write to Permissions, W. W. Norton & Company, Inc., 500 Fifth Avenue, New York, NY 10110

Manufacturing by RR Donnelley, Harrisonburg, VA
Book design by Chris Welch
Production manager: Anna Oler

Library of Congress Cataloging-in-Publication Data

Schlesinger, Arthur Meier, 1917–
War and the American presidency / Arthur M. Schlesinger, Jr.— 1st ed.
p. cm.
Includes index.
ISBN 0-393-06002-0
1. United States—Foreign relations—Philosophy. 2. United States—Foreign relations—2001– 3. Unilateral acts (International law) 4. Iraq War, 2003—Influence. 5. War and emergency powers—United States—History. 6. Presidents—United States—History. 7. Democracy—United States—History. I. Title.
JZ1480.S35 2004
327.1'6'0973—dc22   2004009872

ISBN 0-393-32769-8 pbk.

W. W. Norton & Company, Inc.
500 Fifth Avenue, New York, N.Y. 10110
www.wwnorton.com

W. W. Norton & Company Ltd.
Castle House, 75/76 Wells Street, London W1T 3QT

1 2 3 4 5 6 7 8 9 0

To William vanden Heuvel,
wise, loyal, and generous friend

CONTENTS

FOREWORD

The Iraq War has provoked, or inspired, many excellent books on urgent subjects: the war itself; how we Americans got into it; whether or not we should have got into it; the cast of characters who got us into it. Instant history is useful, and the resulting rebuttals and surrebuttals will produce valuable evidence for future historians.

I believe that the relationship between the Iraq adventure and the national past is also essential to explore. The historical dimension, somewhat neglected in the instant history archive, is indispensable to an understanding of current crises and helpful in clarifying the choices we must make in dealing with them. This book is intended to supply historical background for recent developments and debates in U.S. foreign policy.

Whether we are aware of it or not, the national past colors our reactions to the present. No one is a *tabula rasa*. Americans

are molded by ideas and events they have long since forgotten or never heard of. Our ancestors confronted their own
crises and mostly resolved them—at least the republic has
survived. Their experience is not irrelevant to our concerns
and predicaments.

History pervades the making of decisions. The policy that
we now call "unilateralism" is as old as the republic. Laid
down by George Washington and Thomas Jefferson, it guided
statesmen for more than a century and is still in the DNA of
many Americans. But times change. Given the shrinking
world and the increased vulnerability of the United States,
Woodrow Wilson and Franklin D. Roosevelt came to the
conclusion that the national interest called for processes and
institutions of collective security.

No one thought that the United States should turn over
its national security to multilateral organizations, but collective security seemed a sensible approach to a volatile world.
The elder President Bush, for example, regarded multilater-
alism as a good thing, as he demonstrated in the first Gulf
War. The younger President Bush, however, has unfurled the
historic banner of unilateralism.

And George W. Bush has given unilateralism an unprecedented twist. The Bush Doctrine embraces preventive war as
the basis of U.S. foreign policy. It downplays containment and
deterrence—the combination that won us the Cold War.
Since we arrogate to ourselves the exclusive right to wage
preventive war, we ignore the dark warning of Secretary of
State John Quincy Adams against going abroad "in search of
monsters to destroy." Such a course, Adams said, might make

the United States "the dictatress of the world. She would no longer be the ruler of her own spirit." Given the Bush administration's purposeful drive toward domination of the world, Adams would not have been at all surprised by the wicked things Americans did at Abu Ghraib.

When we initiate war unilaterally, we set the republic up as the world's judge, jury, and executioner. The direct consequence is that never before in American history has the United States been so feared and hated by the rest of the world.

And it all goes for naught: President Bush has rendered the Bush Doctrine obsolete. That doctrine requires near-perfect intelligence about the enemy's intentions and capabilities. Its first application to Iraq shows that our intelligence agencies have a damned long way to go in the quest for accuracy. The credibility gap opened up by the failure to find weapons of mass destruction in Iraq makes a second application of the Bush Doctrine very unlikely. Remember the boy who cried "wolf."

We went to war against Iraq because of presidential reaction to phony intelligence. Thirty years ago in a book called *The Imperial Presidency* I pointed out that war customarily expands presidential power. Then the return of peace emboldens the Congress to restore the constitutional balance between the executive and the legislative branches. After the end of the Civil War, in which James Bryce noted that Abraham Lincoln "wielded more authority than any single Englishman since Oliver Cromwell," it took only three years for Congress to impeach Lincoln's successor. After the end of the Cold War, Congress took seven years to find a second president to impeach. Impeachment is an extreme way of teaching presidents lessons.

Iraq has now resurrected presidential power, and the imperial presidency has been born again, with its usual cavalier attitude toward due process and individual freedom. There are the excesses of the Patriot Act; the administration's contention that a presidential pronouncement of "enemy combatant" can justify suspension of habeas corpus; the Guantánamo prisoners consigned for years to a legal limbo without access to lawyers or families; the many months of indifference to Red Cross reports of cruelties to detainees in Iraq. The resurrection of the imperial presidency has had such negative consequences for civil liberties as to create an improbable coalition between liberals and libertarian conservatives against presidential imperialism redux.

The war in Iraq raises other questions. Is there a moral obligation for a free people to support the president in time of war? If there is such a principle, it has been violated in every war in American history. Not only the American Civil Liberties Union but ex-president Theodore Roosevelt and Senator Robert A. Taft have asserted the right to criticize presidents in wartime. Governments sometimes indulge in hyperpatriotic binges, as in the Alien and Sedition Acts and Attorney General A. Mitchell Palmer's Red Scare. As time passes, we hate ourselves in the morning. History illuminates the true meaning of patriotism in wartime.

What of the tainted election of 2000? That election does not seem to have handicapped President Bush, a tribute to his political skill and shrewdness. But it does mark the fourth time that the people's choice did not make it to the White House—an anomaly in a constitutional democracy. Few Americans understand the electoral college, but history unravels the mystery. I discuss the risks of a direct popular vote for president with the likely effect of producing a gaggle of splinter parties and runoff elections. A possible remedy can assure that the popular-vote winner makes the White House without inviting the destabilization of American politics. That would be a reinforcement of American democracy in troubled times.

But has democracy a future anyway? The world got along without democracy until two centuries ago, and there is little evidence that constitutional democracy is likely to triumph in the century ahead. The failures of democracy in the last century handed the initiative to secular totalitarianism—communism, fascism, Nazism. History was their God, and history failed them. At the start of the twenty-first century democracy finds itself challenged by religious fanatics. God is their God, and heaven's their destination. The search for a democratic alternative is urgent. "Perhaps no form of government," said Bryce, "needs great leaders as much as democracy."

What does history tell us about our ability to predict the future? The book concludes with an analysis of where history helps presidents and where history misleads presidents. This is a question that has always fascinated me as a professional historian and a sometime public official. Clio, the muse of history, remains inscrutable.

My wife, Alexandra Emmet Schlesinger, has endured the

throes of composition with her customary grace, tolerance, and support. I also take much pleasure in thanking Drake McFeely of W. W. Norton for valuable suggestions and his staff, especially Joy Chen and Ann Adelman, for seeing the manuscript through the publishing process. I am indebted to Randy Hutton of Cohen Carruth, Inc. for the index.

Arthur M. Schlesinger, Jr.
May 15, 2004

WAR AND THE
AMERICAN
PRESIDENCY

★

CHAPTER I

UNILATERALISM
The Oldest Doctrine in American
Foreign Policy

Unilateralism?* There is no older American tradition in the conduct of foreign affairs. Two centuries ago, the founding fathers of the infant republic were determined to protect their audacious experiment in self-government from entrapment in foreign quarrels. They insisted on unhampered freedom of action as the cornerstone of foreign policy. George Washington, in his Farewell Address, admonished his countrymen to "steer clear of permanent alliances with any portion of the foreign world." Thomas Jefferson, in his first inaugural, proposed "peace, commerce,

---

*In *The General and the President* (1951), a book about General MacArthur and President Truman, Richard H. Rovere and I wrote, "Unilateralism, to coin one more gobbledygook term, is the new isolationism." In the preface to a 1965 edition, we wrote, "We appear, to our present astonishment, to be making a claim to having given the language the word 'unilateralism.' It hardly seems possible that we deserve any such distinction. All we

and honest friendship with all nations: entangling alliances with none." Hamiltonian Federalists and Jeffersonian Republicans agreed on this, if on little else.

The view that America must be and remain the master of its own fate is conventionally termed "isolationism." In fact, the United States has not been notably isolationist in other than political relationships. It has never been isolationist with regard to commerce. American merchant vessels roamed the Seven Seas from the first days of independence. Nor has it been isolationist with regard to culture. Its explorers, missionaries, writers, artists, scholars, and tourists have ever wandered eagerly about the planet. But through most of its history, America has been stubbornly unilateralist in foreign relations.

Only a direct threat to national safety could justify temporary alliances and participation in foreign wars. Like the British, the United States has regarded the military domination of Europe by a single power as such a threat. Jefferson had been pro-French in the 1790s, but sentiment surrendered to geopolitics and his concern for a "salutary balance" among nations. "It cannot be to our interest," Jefferson observed

---

can say is that, if we do, we are now properly regretful." Were Rovere and I really guilty of coining that gobbledygook term? ("Gobbledygook" itself was coined in 1943 by Maury Maverick to describe the patois of the bureaucracy.) My edition of the *Oxford English Dictionary* throws no light on this momentous question, so I applied to that eminent custodian of the language William Safire, who referred me to the *OED Supplement*, which finds the word used in 1926 and 1935. The next citation was 1959, eight years after *The General and the President*, so Rovere and I perhaps share a measure of guilt for helping put the word in respectable circulation.

when Napoleon bestrode the continent, "that all Europe should be reduced to a single monarchy." America would be forever in danger, he said, should "the whole force of Europe [be] wielded by a single hand."

But between Napoleon and the Kaiser no single forceful hand appeared, and Americans became settled in their determination to avoid ensnarement in the corrupt and corrupting world of European power politics. By the Monroe Doctrine, the United States sought to seal off South America as well, warning European powers against intervention in hemisphere affairs and promising reciprocal American abstention from meddling in European affairs. It was, alas, imperfectly aware of its considerable indebtedness to the British fleet for that happy century of what C. Vann Woodward has called "free security." Free security undergirded American faith in unilateralism. So too did the city-upon-a-hill image of America held by Americans persuaded of the moral superiority of their nation to all other nations.

As American power grew, so did American involvement in the world. Hardly more than a century ago, the Spanish-American War signaled the entry of the United States into great power calculations. Then the First World War revived the Jeffersonian warning. Once again, as in the time of Napoleon, the force of Europe might be wielded by a single hand. A balance of power in Europe served American interests as it had served British interests. Every European war with serious naval operations in the North Atlantic has eventually drawn in the United States. It entered the Great War in its own national interest.

But for President Woodrow Wilson, national interest was not enough to justify the sacrifice and horror of war. His need for a loftier justification led him to offer his country and the world a novel and bold conception. Where Washington and Jefferson had seen independence, Wilson saw interdependence. His aim was to replace the war-breeding alliance system and the bad old balance of power with a "community of power" embodied in a universal League of Nations. The establishment of the League, Wilson said, promised a peaceful future. Should this promise not be kept, Wilson warned in Omaha in September 1919, "I can predict with absolute certainty that within another generation there will be another world war."

For a glorious moment, Wilson was the world's prophet of peace. No other American president—not Lincoln, not FDR, not JFK, not Reagan—has ever enjoyed the international acclaim that engulfed Wilson. But Wilson was a prophet without much honor in his own country. His vision of a community of power implied a world of law. It rested on the collective prevention and punishment of aggression. Article X of the League covenant imposed on member nations the "obligation" to "preserve against external aggression the territorial integrity and existing political independence of all members of the league." This meant, or seemed to mean, that American troops might be sent into combat not just in defense of the United States but in defense of world order. U.S. soldiers would have to kill and die for what many would regard as an abstraction and do so when the life of their own nation was not in danger.

The commitment of troops to combat became the perennial obstacle to American acceptance of the Wilsonian dream. It is a *political* obstacle: how to explain to the American people why their husbands, fathers, brothers, sons should die in conflicts in remote lands where the local outcome makes no direct difference to the United States? And it is a *constitutional* obstacle: how to reconcile the provision in the U.S. Constitution giving Congress exclusive power to declare war with the dispatch of American troops into hostilities at the behest of a collective security organization?

Wilson's fight for the League of Nations foundered in the Senate on these obstacles. It foundered too because Wilson seemed to make the League an executive branch project, thereby neglecting the Senate, the constitutional body authorized to approve treaties; and it foundered because Wilson seemed to make the League a party project, thereby alienating internationalist Republicans. So America, after the two-year Wilsonian internationalist binge, reverted by 1920 to familiar and comforting unilateralism.

Warren G. Harding, Wilson's successor in the White House, announced the return to the old-time religion in his inaugural address. "In a deliberate questioning of a suggested change in national policy, where internationality was to supersede nationality," Harding said, "we turned to a referendum, to the American people." There had been ample discussion, and the result was a clear public mandate.

America, our America, the America builded on the foundation laid by the inspired fathers, can be a party to no permanent military alliance. It can enter into no political commitments, nor assume any economic obligations which will subject our decisions to any other than our own authority. . . . Confident of our ability to work out our own destiny, and jealously guarding our right to do so, we seek no part in directing the destinies of the Old World. We do not mean to be entangled. We will accept no responsibility except as our own conscience and judgment, in each instance, may determine. . . .

A world supergovernment is contrary to everything we cherish and can have no sanction by our Republic. . . . It is not suspicion of others, it is patriotic adherence to the things which made us what we are.

Disenchantment over the Great War accelerated the return to the womb. Revisionist historians portrayed American entry into the war as a disastrous mistake brought about by sinister forces—international bankers, munitions makers, British propagandists—and by Wilsonian deceptions and delusions. Novelists and playwrights depicted the sacrifice of war as meaningless. The onset of the Great Depression further confirmed the isolationist retreat.

Young Franklin Roosevelt as assistant secretary of the Navy had been an early and ardent advocate of American intervention in the First World War and thereafter of American entry into the League of Nations. He was thirty-eight years old when the U.S. Senate rejected the Treaty of Versailles in 1920; he was only fifty-seven years old when war broke out in Europe in 1939. During the interwar years the struggle against isolationism had consumed much of his time and energy. He believed, as he said in 1919, that America had "taken on for all time a new relationship" to the world; it would commit a grievous wrong to itself and to all mankind "if it were ever to attempt to go backwards towards an old Chinese wall policy of isolationism." "If the World War showed anything more than another," he said during his vice presidential campaign in 1920, "it showed the American people the futility of imagining that they could live in smug content their lives in their own way while the rest of the world burned in the conflagration of war across the ocean." As foreign policy spokesman for the Democratic Party, he declared in a *Foreign Affairs* article in 1928 that only by acts of international collaboration could the United States "regain the world's trust and friendship and become again of service."

But in these years he witnessed the fierce revival of isolationism in the traditional American sense—that is, insistence on national freedom of action, on abstention from "entangling alliances," on unilateralism in the conduct of foreign affairs. In time the bitter reaction against the American involvement in the First World War engulfed Roosevelt himself. By 1932, he abandoned the League as a lost cause. Isolationism set the terms of the foreign policy debate. Roosevelt had no illusions about the threats to peace posed by Nazi Germany and Imperial Japan. Although he was a mighty domestic president, he could not, for all his popularity and all his wiles, control an isolationist Congress when it came to foreign policy. Congress rejected American membership in the World Court. It passed rigid neutrality legislation that, by denying the president authority to discriminate between aggressor and victim, nullified any American role in restraining aggression. In sum, it put American foreign policy in a straitjacket during the critical years before the Second World War.

We sometimes forget how brief an interval separated the two world wars. The generation that ruled Washington in the 1940s had cut its political teeth in the Wilson administration. The experience of a glorious internationalist moment followed by a passionate isolationist revival had engraved itself indelibly on the consciousness of the old Wilsonians. The great fear that haunted FDR's generation was the fear of resurgent American isolationism.

Roosevelt meanwhile began a campaign of popular education to awaken the nation to international dangers. In 1939, the outbreak of war in Europe fulfilled Wilson's Omaha prediction and justified Roosevelt's warning. But it did not destroy isolationism. Rather, it ushered in the most savage national debate of my lifetime. The debate between interventionists and isolationists in 1940–41 had an inner fury that tore apart families, friends, churches, universities, and political parties. As late as August 1941, the extension of the draft passed the House by only a single vote.

Pearl Harbor settled that particular debate. But in vindicating internationalism, it did not vanquish isolationism. This was shown in 1942 when internationalists of both parties using a hit list of isolationist legislators worked to elect a "win-the-war" Congress. In FDR's own congressional district, internationalist Republicans like Wendell Willkie and Thomas E. Dewey opposed the renomination of the bitter isolationist Hamilton Fish, but Fish won the primary by two to one. In the general election, only 5 of 115 congressmen with isolationist records were beaten. The Republicans gained forty-four seats in the House and nine in the Senate—their best performance in many years. After the election Willkie's candidate for the national chairmanship of the Republican Party lost to Harrison Spangler, a prewar isolationist who had backed the isolationist leader Senator Robert A. Taft in the Republican convention in 1940. Secretary of State Cordell Hull told Vice President Henry Wallace that "the country was going in exactly the same steps it followed in 1918." Hull, Wallace noted, thought it "utterly important to keep the sequence of events from following the 1918–1921 pattern because he felt if we went into isolationism this time, the world was lost."

For Roosevelt, the critical task in 1943–45, beyond winning the war, was to commit the United States to postwar international structures before peace could return the nation to its old bad habits. The memory, still vivid, of the repudiation of the League two decades before suggested that the task would not be easy. Isolationism had been the American norm for a century and a half; internationalism had been a two-year Wilsonian aberration. No one could assume that isolationism would simply drift away. It had to be brought to a definitive end by American commitments to an international order. But Roosevelt was a careful politician; and he proceeded to lay the groundwork in 1943–45 with the same circumspection with which he had steered the nation away from isolationism in 1937–41.

Roosevelt moved steadily but carefully to make the case for postwar internationalism. "There have always been cheerful idiots in this country," he said in a Christmas Eve fireside chat after his return from the Teheran summit in 1943, "who believed that there would be no more war for us if everybody in America would only return into their homes and lock their front doors behind them." At a dinner of the Foreign Policy Association in October 1944, three months before he left for Yalta, he said that "enduring peace in the world has not a chance unless this Nation—our America—is willing to cooperate in winning it and maintaining it." If the Republicans took Congress in the impending presidential election, he pointed out, the veteran isolationist Hiram Johnson would become chairman of the Senate Foreign Relations Committee. Hamilton Fish would become chairman of the powerful House Committee on Rules. "Can anyone suppose that these isolationists have changed their minds about world affairs? . . . Politicians who embraced the policy of isolationism, and who never raised their voices against it in our days of peril—I don't think they are reliable custodians of the future of America." He said privately, "Anybody who thinks that isolationism is dead in this country is crazy. As soon as this war is over, it may well be stronger than ever."

Roosevelt won his fourth term in November 1944. But the margin of victory (53.5 percent) was the narrowest of his four elections—indeed, the narrowest by which any president had been elected since 1916. Congress, which had been fractious enough during the war, gave every promise of being more fractious than ever as war's end approached. In

December 1944, a Washington diplomatic correspondent warned the new secretary of state, Edward Stettinius, of a "revolt against the Administration now developing in the Senate" by a group of twenty-seven senators, including Senator Walter George of Georgia, an important Democrat. "They propose," Stettinius was told, "to take the position that American foreign policy should be formulated and carried out only with the advice and consent of the Senate, and they propose to exert their rights in this respect more and more positively as time goes on."

Roosevelt moved methodically to prepare the American people for a continuing world role. In doing so, he took care to avoid Wilson's mistakes. He involved leading senators and internationalist Republicans in postwar planning. He organized a series of conferences setting up international machinery to deal with the problems of peace, and did so before the war ended. These conferences, held mostly at American initiative and dominated mostly by American agendas, came up with postwar blueprints for international organization (Dumbarton Oaks); finance, trade, and development (Bretton Woods); food and agriculture (Hot Springs); civil aviation (Chicago); relief and reconstruction (Washington). Above all, Roosevelt saw the United Nations, as Charles E. Bohlen wrote in his memoirs, as "the only device that could keep the United States from slipping back into isolationism." He was determined to put the United Nations in business while the war was still on and the American people were still in an internationalist mood; hence the founding conference in San Francisco, which took place after his death but before victory.

Once again, there arose the Article X question that had so bedeviled Wilson. Could the new United Nations on its own order American troops into war in defense of world order and the peace system? Washington's veto in the Security Council ensured that U.S. soldiers could not be sent into combat over a president's objection. But if a president favored U.S. participation in a UN collective security action, must he go to Congress for specific authorization? Or could the UN Charter supersede the U.S. Constitution?

The UN Participation Act of 1945 came up with an ingenious solution. It authorized the United States to commit limited force through congressionally approved special agreements as provided for in Article 43 of the UN Charter. Presidents could not enter into such agreements on their own. If more force was required than the agreement specified, the president must return to Congress for further authorization. This formula offered a convincing way to reconcile the charter and the Constitution. Unfortunately, the Article 43 special agreement procedure soon withered on the vine. When Harry S. Truman sent troops into Korea five years later, he sought neither an Article 43 agreement nor a congressional joint resolution, thereby setting the precedent that persuaded several successors that presidents possess the inherent power to go to war whenever they choose.

The postwar reversion to isolationism, so much feared by Roosevelt and his generation, obviously did not take place— or, to put it more accurately, did not take place at once. Within a few years after the end of the war, the Truman Doctrine, the Marshall Plan, NATO and other security pacts, along with far-flung military, naval, and air deployments, bound the United States to the outside world in a way that isolationists, in their most pessimistic moments, could hardly have envisaged. In two hot wars fought on the mainland of East Asia under the sanction of the Cold War, the United States lost nearly 100,000 people. Even the traditionally isolationist Republican Party joined for a season in support of collective action. At last, it seemed, Americans had made the great turning and would forever after accept international responsibilities. The age of American isolationism, it was supposed, was finally over.

Viewed through the prism of the twenty-first century, that appears an illusion. It is now surely clear that the upsurge in American internationalism during the Cold War was a reaction to what was seen as the direct and urgent Soviet threat to the security of the United States. In Jeffersonian terms, it was a reaction to the fear that the whole force of Europe might be wielded by a single hand. It is to Joseph Stalin that Americans owe the forty-year suppression of the unilateral impulse.

The collapse of the Soviet threat revived the prospect that haunted Roosevelt over half a century ago—a return to isolationism. This suggestion requires immediate qualification. The United States will never—unless Pat Buchanan makes it to the White House—return to the classical isolationism of no entangling alliances. In the present world, a world in which we are irreversibly entangled by economic and cultural ties as well as by geopolitical imperatives, classical isolationism is an impossible dream. The United States will continue to accept international political, economic, and military commitments unprecedented in its history. It will even enlarge some, as it did NATO. But such enlargement hinges on the assumption that other nations will do as America tells them. The isolationist impulse has risen from the grave in what has always been its essential program—unilateralism.

The Clinton administration began in the 1990s by basing its foreign policy on the premise that the United States could not solve the world's troubles all by itself. The end of the Cold War, it was expected, would free the United Nations, so long immobilized by the antagonism between the Soviet Union and the Western democracies, to realize the aims of the men of San Francisco. "Many of our most important objectives," said Warren Christopher, President Clinton's first secretary of state, "cannot be achieved without the cooperation of others." The key to the future, in the early Clintonian view, was collective action through the building of international institutions.

But as the Soviet threat faded away, the incentives for international collaboration faded away too. The Republican capture of Congress in 1994 gave unilateralism a new force and momentum. House Speaker Newt Gingrich accused Clinton of cherishing a "multinational fantasy" and a wish "to subordinate the United States to the United Nations." Even a moderate Republican such as Bob Dole, the Republican presidential candidate in 1996, observed that international organizations too often "reflect a consensus that opposes American interests or does not reflect American principles and ideals." Sir Nicholas Henderson, the distinguished former

British ambassador to Washington, soon lamented "the rejection by the Republicans of the main plank of US foreign policy of the last 50 years."

The culmination of resurgent unilateralism was—and is—the campaign against the United Nations. The United Nations was an American vision propelled onto the world scene by two American presidents. Yet today it is under unrelenting attack in the house of the founders. The Republican Congress, denouncing the UN as bloated, wasteful, and disobedient, long withheld large sums owed to it by the United States and sought to cripple the international organization in manifold ways. Bills are even introduced in Congress calling for the United States' withdrawal from the United Nations.

Far beyond Washington, in the crazier parts of our bewildered and bewildering country, right-wing fanatics anxiously scan the sky watching for black helicopters transporting a UN army that intends, they believe, to take away their guns and their liberties and impose, in the words of one of them, "a world government with unlimited power over the whole world."

Let me not give an exaggerated impression. Hard-line unilateralism falls far short of commanding a national majority. Public opinion polls show that most Americans support the UN. Most Americans favor greater involvement in UN peacekeeping operations, favor a standing UN peace force, even favor increased spending on foreign economic aid. Support for international institutions is especially strong among opinionmakers and among thoughtful persons in both parties. Nevertheless, the support, while sincere enough, is weak compared with the ferocity of the UN's enemies. Pollsters have not discovered satisfactory ways of measuring the intensity factor, which is very often decisive. Moreover, even UN sympathizers draw back at the thought of sending troops abroad to kill and die in the absence of a direct and palpable threat to U.S. vital interests. How to persuade the housewife in Xenia, Ohio, that her husband, brother, or son should die in Bosnia or Somalia or Iraq or some other remote place where vital U.S. interests are not involved? Nor is it just the Xenia housewife who must be persuaded. How many stalwart internationalists in the Council on Foreign Relations are sending their own sons to die in Iraq?

Let no one doubt the political potency of the unilateralist resuscitation, strengthened as it is by America's post–Cold War position as the planet's sole superpower and by the consequent reduction in international checks and balances. Unilateralism rose to crescendo in the Bush Doctrine of the right to wage preventive war, a right reserved exclusively for the United States. The Bush Doctrine, however, also demonstrated the limits of unilateralism. Once the going got tough in Iraq, the Bush administration tried to dump the mess of its own making on the United Nations, heretofore an object of contempt in Bush's Washington.

The notion that internationalists propose to turn over the foreign relations of the United States to the UN is, of course, fatuous. The existence of the UN does not abolish the basic dynamics of international politics—national interest and the search for stable balances of power. The United States, and other nations, will not surrender the freedom to protect vital interests. But the UN and other international bodies supply arenas where clashes of interest and power can be contained, refined, and harmonized.

The United States, as it seeks to advance its national interests, will increasingly discover, I believe, that joint action may often be the best way to safeguard those interests. The twenty-first century will be turbulent and chaotic for a long time to come—a world of inconceivable poverty, exploding population, desperate inequalities, mass migrations, fanatical ethnic and religious animosities, artificial frontiers, continuing arms flows, angry competition for resources, disintegration of traditional structures, and instantaneous communication of hopes and grievances.

In such a world, as that admirable international civil servant Sir Brian Urquhart has said, "No one nation, or even a partnership of two or three nations, is going to be able to assume the role of world arbitrator and policeman, even if we suppose the other nations would accept it, which they are most unlikely to do. The United Nations, therefore, must be brought to maturity to take that task." The UN, after all, is a useful way to pool knowledge, share burdens, and distribute blame. For all its defects, a world without the UN would be considerably more troublesome.

The future of American unilateralism? The United States is the only military, economic, scientific, technological, and cultural superpower on the planet; but that does not mean that its leaders are omnipotent and omniscient. Military might is no substitute for friends and allies, nor is it a substitute for wisdom. It is a stimulus to vainglory—and vain glory is self-defeating, as we Americans are learning the hard way. In due course the failures of unilateralism will teach us to meet the problems that assail us by working with other nations and using and strengthening international institutions.

CHAPTER 2

EYELESS IN IRAQ
The Bush Doctrine and
Its Consequences

Unilateralism reached its grand climax when President George W. Bush made a fatal change in the foreign policy of the United States. He repudiated the strategy that won the Cold War—the combination of containment and deterrence carried out through such multilateral agencies as the UN, NATO, and the Organization of American States. The Bush Doctrine reverses all that. The essence of our new strategy is military: to strike a potential enemy, unilaterally if necessary, before he has a chance to strike us. War, traditionally a matter of last resort, becomes a matter of presidential choice.

This is a revolutionary change. Mr. Bush replaced a policy aimed at peace through the prevention of war by a policy aimed at peace through preventive war. He did this quietly, smoothly, and skillfully, without calling undue attention to so fundamental a revision of foreign policy or provoking a national debate over his drastic change of course.

The combination of containment and deterrence was initiated over half a century ago by President Truman. It was confirmed as a bipartisan policy by President Eisenhower and thereafter sustained by Presidents Kennedy, Johnson, Nixon (with modifications), Carter, Reagan (with deviations), George H. W. Bush, and Clinton. During the long years of the Cold War, preventive war was unmentionable. Its advocates were regarded as loonies.

In the Truman administration, Francis P. Matthews, a secretary of the Navy, called publicly for war on the Soviet Union as a way to compel cooperation for peace. He was immediately rebuked by the president. "I have always been opposed, even to the thought of such a war," Truman wrote in his *Memoirs*. "There is nothing more foolish than to think that war can be stopped by war. You don't 'prevent' anything by war except peace."

In 1954, James Reston of the *New York Times* asked President Dwight Eisenhower in a press conference what he thought of preventive war. "A preventive war, to my mind, is an impossibility," Eisenhower said. ". . . I don't believe there is such a thing, and frankly I wouldn't even listen to anyone seriously that came in and talked about such a thing."

In 1962, when the Kennedy administration was wrestling with the threat of Soviet nuclear missiles in Cuba, the Joint Chiefs of Staff recommended removing the missiles by preventive attack. Robert Kennedy called the Joint Chiefs' idea "Pearl Harbor in reverse." He added, "For 75 years we had not been that kind of country." President Bush, it seems, would like to make us that kind of country today.

Looking back over the forty years of the Cold War, we can be everlastingly grateful that the loonies on both sides were powerless. By 2003, however, they ran the Pentagon, and preventive war—the Bush Doctrine—is now official policy. Sixty years ago, the Japanese anticipated the Bush Doctrine in their attack on the U.S. Navy at Pearl Harbor. This was, Franklin D. Roosevelt observed, an exploit that would live in infamy—except now, evidently, when employed by the United States.

Given the disrepute attached to the idea of "preventive" war, the Bush administration prefers to talk about "preemptive" war, and too many have followed its example. The distinction between "preemptive" and "preventive" is well worth preserving. It is the distinction between legality and illegality. "Preemptive" war refers to a direct, immediate, specific threat that must be crushed at once; in the words of the Department of Defense manual, "an attack initiated on the basis of incontrovertible evidence that an enemy attack is imminent." "Preventive" war refers to potential, future, therefore speculative threats.

"Daniel Webster," Condoleezza Rice, President Bush's national security adviser, informed the White House press, "actually wrote a very famous defense of anticipatory self-defense." Dr. Rice, the former provost of Stanford, does not know her American history. Secretary of State Webster's "famous" 1841 statement was that preemptive reaction could be justified *only* if the attacker showed "a necessity of self-defense, instant, overwhelming, leaving no choice of means, and no moment for deliberation." Preventive war has no such claim to legitimacy. It is founded on prophecy, a dubious source.

The rise of international terrorism underlies the Bush administration's shift from containment plus deterrence to preventive war as the basis of U.S. policy. The Cold War, after all, was an old-fashioned rivalry among sovereign states, visible entities with governments accountable for their decisions. But international terrorists are invisible and unaccountable. They strike from the shadows and recede into the shadows. International terrorism consequently calls for new strategies.

In his West Point speech of June 1, 2002, Mr. Bush explicitly rejected containment and deterrence as sufficient weapons for the war against terrorism. "We must," he said, "take the battle to the enemy . . . and confront the worst threats before they emerge. In the world we have entered, the only path to safety is the path of action. And this nation will act." On July 19 that year, at Fort Drum, New York, he said again: "America must act against these terrible threats before they're fully formed."

Such speeches prepared the way for a formal statement, *The National Security Strategy of the United States of America*, issued by the White House in September 2002. "Given the goals of rogue states and terrorists," this document says,

> the United States can no longer solely rely on a reactive posture as we have in the past. The inability to deter a potential attacker, the immediacy of today's threats, and

the magnitude of potential harm that could be caused by our adversaries' choice of weapons, do not permit that option. We cannot let our enemies strike first.

In addition to police and CIA methods of combating international terrorism, *The National Security Strategy* calls for the initiation of military action by far vaguer and looser standards than those laid down by Daniel Webster. Actually, the only serious application of U.S. force thus far has been an old-fashioned attack on a sovereign state. The war against Iraq was not preemptive. It was not a war "initiated on the basis of incontrovertible evidence that an enemy attack is imminent." Far from that: the CIA analysts, according to George Tenet, the CIA director, "never said there was an imminent threat." The war on Iraq was a *preventive* war.

Where did Mr. Bush get the revolutionary idea of preventive war as the basis of U.S. foreign policy? His conviction apparently is that the unique position of the United States as the planet's supreme military, economic, and cultural power creates an unprecedented opportunity for America to impose its values on other countries and thereby save them from themselves. Our supremacy, rendered permanent, will enable us to promote democracy, free markets, private enterprise, and godliness, and thereby control the future.

The case for global hegemony through unilateral action was first presented in 1992 in a mysterious Pentagon paper apparently approved by Paul Wolfowitz and Dick Cheney and rapidly suppressed by the Bush I administration. Wolfowitz opposed President Bush's 1991 decision not to press on to

Baghdad and get rid of Saddam Hussein forever. In 1996, a document prepared by Richard Perle, Douglas Feith, and half a dozen others for Benjamin Netanyahu, the Israeli hard-liner, called for, among other things, a "focus on removing Saddam Hussein from power in Iraq"—a thought that hard-liners considered to be much in the Israeli interest. In 1998, Donald Rumsfeld, Wolfowitz, and Perle were among the eighteen signers of an open letter to President Clinton argu-ing that regime change in Iraq "needs to become the aim of American foreign policy."

America Unbound (2004), by Ivo H. Daalder and James M. Lindsay, two Brookings Institution political scientists, is a use-ful analysis of what the authors term "the Bush revolution in foreign policy." Their approach is clinical, incisive, and work-manlike. Their emphasis is less on the shift to preventive war than on the administration's doctrinaire unilateralism and its moralistic arrogance.

Daalder and Lindsay see two sets of presidential advisers united in immediate policy but divided in ultimate objec-tives. One set consists of the now-all-too-familiar "neo-cons"—Paul Wolfowitz, Richard Perle, Douglas Feith, Lewis Libby, Elliott Abrams, and, outside the government, William Kristol, Robert Kagan, Charles Krauthammer, and Joshua Muravchik. The second is led by the "assertive nationalists"— Vice President Dick Cheney and Defense Secretary Donald Rumsfeld. The neocons are visionaries who want to remake the world in the American image; the assertive nationalists are hard-boiled politicians who want to use American power to intimidate rival nations and to crush potential threats to

American security and to corporate enterprise. Both factions are allied in their contempt for international institutions and their advocacy of preventive war.

They also agreed that regime change in Baghdad should be a top priority in our foreign policy. Ten days into the Bush presidency, the first meeting of the Bush National Security Council concentrated on Iraq. "Getting Hussein was now the administration's focus," Secretary of the Treasury Paul O'Neill concluded, "that much was already clear." Seven months later, al-Qaeda terrorists smashed into the World Trade Center and the Pentagon. The logical response was to invade Afghanistan and destroy Osama bin Laden and his protectors, the Taliban regime. This course was indeed pursued, but it soon yielded priority to Saddam Hussein and Iraq. That was the moment the neocons and the assertive nationalists around Bush II had been waiting a decade for.

Rumsfeld and Wolfowitz, who regarded Iraq as unfinished business left over from Bush I's administration, lost no time in placing Iraq as the top priority on the presidential agenda. Rumsfeld favored war on Iraq because he had convinced himself that Saddam Hussein actively possessed weapons of mass destruction, that Saddam Hussein was actively allied with Osama bin Laden, and that the transfer of America's Middle East military base from unstable and two-faced Saudi Arabia to compliant Iraq was desirable.

Wolfowitz believed those three things and, in addition, cherished the neoconservative fantasy that establishing Jeffersonian democracy in Iraq could modernize and democratize the entire Muslim world, which would then be less hostile to Israel. In an interview with Sam Tanenhaus published in *Vanity Fair* (June 2003), Wolfowitz listed the imagined weapons of mass destruction and the imagined partnership with al-Qaeda as the two compelling reasons to go to war against Iraq. He added a third reason—the liberation of the long-suffering people of Iraq from a monstrous tyrant. But, he said, that by itself was "not a reason to put American kids' lives at risk."

Now that evidence of weapons of mass destruction (WMDs) and proof of collaboration between Saddam Hussein and Osama bin Laden have failed to materialize, the Bush administration is left with liberation, which it had once deemed an insufficient justification for putting American lives at risk. Nonetheless, it is a powerful argument. Had the government followed the policy that many Americans, including this writer, advocated, the policy of containment and deterrence, the policy of putting Saddam Hussein "in a box," he would possibly still be in power in Baghdad. This is an unsettling thought for opponents of the war. However, there are a lot of bad guys in the world. Is the United States obliged to eliminate them all?

Still, why did Mr. Bush and his close advisers decide to go to war against Iraq? The pretext was that Saddam Hussein was a mortal danger to the peace. The administration drew a terrifying picture of an Iraq bristling with weapons of mass destruction, soon to acquire nuclear bombs, and closely allied with Osama bin Laden and al-Qaeda.

No doubt they genuinely believed it. I was an intelligence officer during the Second World War, and I noticed the alacrity with which I disseminated intelligence that benefited my political agenda (support for non-Communist resistance groups)—the sin now known as "cherry-picking." Dissatisfied with the cautious assessments emanating from the State Department and CIA, the neocons set up an Office of Special Plans in the Pentagon, which produced, with the enthusiastic cooperation of Iraqi defectors, intelligence far more to their liking.

They also brought heavy pressure on CIA analysts, as shown by Cheney's frequent appearances at CIA headquarters and by the requests of neocon officials for "raw" (i.e., unevaluated) intelligence. David Kay, who headed the unavailing search for WMDs, said that the "caveats" in CIA reports "tended to drop off as the reports would go up the food chain."

The supposition that the Bush people truly believed in their WMD nightmare was indicated by the unconditional quality of their prose. Phrases like "we do know, with absolute certainty," uttered with majestic authority, abounded in Vice President Cheney's speeches. He was also a "no doubt" man, as in, "There is no doubt that Saddam Hussein now has weapons of mass destruction." The president was another "no doubt" man: "Intelligence gathered by this and other governments leaves no doubt that the Iraq regime continues to possess and conceal some of the most lethal weapons ever devised." Asked about the location of the WMDs, Secretary of Defense Rumsfeld said confidently: "We know where they are."

But how could Saddam Hussein use these lethal weapons against his neighbors (he lacked missiles to reach the United States) without inviting and legitimizing punishment by the

international community? If Saddam Hussein were to com-
mit an overt act of aggression, he would play into President
Bush's hands. Therefore he had committed none for a decade.
He was definitely not a clear and present danger to the
United States or anyone else, save his own people.

Why, then, the war on Iraq? It was not to stop international
terrorism; it represented a detour from the war on terrorism
and ended by breeding more terrorists. It was not to save the
peace from Saddam Hussein; he was safely in the box. I don't
think that Mr. Bush went to war in order to gratify the
Halliburton Company or to please Israel or to avenge the
attempted assassination of his father. These may have been
fringe benefits, but he is a president who exults in big ideas.
Perhaps he thinks that his father committed two fatal errors
that led to defeat for reelection in 1992 and that the son is
determined not to repeat. One error was the elder Bush's
alienation of the ideological right. The other was his flippant
dismissal of what he called "the vision thing." The son told
Bob Woodward, "I will seize the opportunity to achieve big
goals." I suspect that he dreams of making his place in history
by converting the Arab world to representative democracy.

"A new regime in Iraq," he said in February 2003, "would
serve as a dramatic and inspiring example of freedom for
other nations in the region." This may explain the reversal by
which the war against Iraq replaced the war against al-Qaeda
as the Bush administration's top priority. Senator Bob
Graham of Florida was the only aspirant for the Democratic
nomination to join Robert Byrd, Edward Kennedy, and
twenty other senators in voting against the resolution author-

izing Bush to attack Iraq. As chairman of the Senate
Intelligence Committee, Graham said he had seen no evidence for the alleged partnership between Saddam Hussein,
a militantly secular Muslim, and Osama bin Laden, a fanatical Muslim fundamentalist. (Observers noted that Saddam
Hussein practically always appeared in Western suits, Osama
bin Laden always in Arab costume. They noted, too, that
when Osama went into hiding, no one supposed for a
moment that he had sought refuge in the country of his
alleged pal and partner, Saddam Hussein. Actually, he seems
to have sought refuge near or in the country of the American
pal General Pervez Musharraf, president of Pakistan.)

There were two quite separate U.S. wars—a war on terrorism, symbolized by Osama bin Laden; a war on Iraq, symbolized by Saddam Hussein. I would have given the Afghan war
the highest priority. Had we done so, we very likely would
have smashed al-Qaeda and captured Osama. Mr. Bush pre-
ferred the war on Iraq. Since he is president and I am not, his
preference won out. The war on Iraq meant an overwhelming diversion of attention, resources, troops, and military
might from the war on terrorism. Far from striking a blow
against terrorism, Mr. Bush's victory over Saddam Hussein
has produced a new generation of terrorists. We know today
that Senator Graham's forebodings, which received little
notice by the media pundits when he expressed them, have
been duly vindicated.

The neocon vision of converting the Islamic world to the
American way of life has waned. George Bush the elder was
generally held to have a vision deficit, but that's not the same

thing as defective vision. The elder Bush was a moderate as president, and he did not notably harm the republic. Indeed, Bush II's vision-free father had a far more accurate forecast of what an American invasion of Iraq might entail. In the book he wrote with General Brent Scowcroft, *A World Transformed* (1998), Bush I defended his decision not to advance to Baghdad in the 1991 Gulf War. "Trying to eliminate Saddam . . . would have incurred incalculable human and political costs," the first President Bush said.

> . . . We would have been forced to occupy Baghdad and, in effect, rule Iraq. . . . There was no viable "exit strategy" we could see, violating another of our principles. Furthermore, we had been self-consciously trying to set a pattern for handling aggression in the post–Cold War world. Going in and occupying Iraq, thus unilaterally exceeding the United Nations' mandate, would have destroyed the precedent of international response to aggression that we hoped to establish.

Bush the elder summed up his view as a stinging sentence: "Had we gone the invasion route, the United States could conceivably still be an occupying power in a bitterly hostile land."

"Once you've got Baghdad, it's not clear what you do with it," the elder Bush's secretary of defense said in 1991. "It's not clear what kind of government you would put in. . . . How much credibility is the government going to have if it's set up by the United States military? . . . To have American military forces engaged in a civil war inside Iraq would fit the definition of quagmire, and we have absolutely no desire to get bogged down in that fashion." The speaker was a younger, wiser, and pre-Halliburton Dick Cheney.

For many months, however, President Bush's extraordinary reversal of the direction of American foreign policy had little effective opposition, or even debate. Why should this have been? After all, nothing in a democracy demands more searching discussion than the choice between peace and war. But voters rallied round the flag after September 11, 2001, because Americans felt, as never before, personal vulnerability to enemy attack. In this "homeland security" mood, Democrats believed that criticism of the president's policies might be mistaken for a deficiency of patriotism.

I think the press and television are also to be blamed for the absence of debate. Editorial pages of our most distinguished newspapers were shamefully—and incredibly—oblivious to the drastic significance of the shift to preventive war as the basis of American foreign policy. Comments by Cheney and Rumsfeld were given top billing in most American papers, even the *New York Times*, while reasoned speeches by Edward Kennedy and Robert Byrd opposing the rush to preventive war were consigned to a paragraph on the back pages or wholly ignored. A philanthropist had to pay the *Times* to print the full text of Byrd's powerful February 12, 2003, speech against the war in a full-page advertisement on March 9.

News stories in the *Times* and elsewhere featured revelations about weapons of mass destruction obligingly supplied by Iraqi exiles, favored in the Pentagon, but dismissed by CIA and State as con men. Like the politicians, the media were fearful of being deemed unpatriotic. In the run-up to war, the media, including the *New York Times* and *The Washington Post*, swallowed whole Colin Powell's February 5, 2003, speech to the United Nations. Skeptics about Iraqi WMDs received little play. The failure to give equal time to the opponents of preventive war discouraged any national debate about the Bush Doctrine.

Moreover, a *Washington Post* poll taken in August 2003 reported that 69 percent of Americans still believed Saddam Hussein was "personally involved" in the attack on the World Trade Center. Where did they get that idea? Perhaps from the administration's rhetoric as filtered through the press. Saddam Hussein is a great villain, but he had nothing to do with the attack on the twin towers, as Mr. Bush belatedly admitted on September 17, 2003.

And we must not underrate President Bush's capacity for getting his way. He is a minority president who lost the popular election by more than half a million votes. The first minority president, John Quincy Adams, also a president's son, said apologetically in his inaugural address: "Less possessed of your confidence, in advance, than any of my predecessors, I am deeply conscious of the prospect that I shall stand more and oftener in need of your indulgence." There were no such apologies in Mr. Bush's inaugural address. He acted as if he had won in a landslide and had earned an electoral mandate—and he got away with it.

For all his buffoonish side, the president is secure in himself, disciplined, decisive, and crafty, and capable of concentrating on a few priorities. He has maintained control of a rag-tag Republican coalition, well described by Kevin Phillips (author of *The Emerging Republican Majority*, 1969) as consisting of "Wall Street, Big Energy, multinational corporations, the Military-Industrial Complex, the Religious Right, the Market Extremist think-tanks, and the Rush Limbaugh Axis." All these groups agree in their strong support of their president, though they sharply disagree among themselves.

President Bush radiates a serene but scary certitude when confronted with complicated problems or disagreements. "There is no doubt in my mind we're doing the right thing," he told Bob Woodward. "Not one doubt." Unlike Tony Blair, "I haven't suffered doubt." Friends attribute this serenity to his religious faith. Woodward, who interviewed Mr. Bush for nearly four hours for his book *Bush at War*, came away with the clear impression that "the president was casting his mission and that of the country in the grand vision of God's master plan." "I'm here for a reason," Mr. Bush told Karl Rove, his political wizard, "and this is going to be how we're going to be judged." A senior aide commented that the president "really believes he was placed here to do this as part of a divine plan." When Woodward asked him whether he consulted his father on the war, Bush replied, "He is the wrong father to appeal to in terms of strength. There is a higher father that I appeal to."

Though there is no doubting the sincerity of Mr. Bush's religious beliefs, his faith also serves his political purposes. Religious statistics are notoriously unreliable, but perhaps a fourth of Americans are born-again, evangelical Christians. In my youth, Protestant fundamentalists could be depended upon to be anti-Catholic and anti-Semitic. They led the campaign against Al Smith in 1928 and John F. Kennedy in 1960. They had lynched Leo Frank in Georgia in 1915. In those days, fundamentalists were a disdained and isolated Bible Belt minority. But in the last generation the evangelical right has formed an alliance with right-wing Catholics over abortion and an alliance with right-wing Jews over the Holy Land. In consequence, they are a far more potent political force today, perhaps affecting more than 40 percent of the electorate; they give a born-again president a built-in advantage.

As Eisenhower's scrambled syntax misled people about his executive determination and political skills, so Mr. Bush's scrambled syntax misleads people, especially liberal intellectuals. The late Murray Kempton was among the first liberals to spot Ike's well-concealed political prowess—"devious" in the best sense of the word, as Nixon said. In an article in *Time*, "The Power of One," Michael Kinsley correctly diagnoses Mr. Bush as "the real thing: a leader." This is certainly not to suggest that Mr. Bush has the weight of experience and the circumspection of judgment that characterized Ike. But he is skillful at mobilizing opinion and brushing aside opposition.

Daalder and Lindsay agree with Kinsley:

> George Bush assumed the presidency with many people openly questioning his ability to master foreign policy. By any reasonable standard, he proved his doubters wrong. . . . To an extent that surprised even his most ardent supporters, he was decisive, resolute, and in command of his advisers.

The preventive war against Iraq was a war of President Bush's choice. It was not, like the Second World War, forced upon the United States. It was not, like the Korean War, the first Gulf War, and the war against the Taliban, a response to overt acts of aggression. Nor did the United States drag itself incrementally into full-scale war, as in Vietnam. The professional military kept its enthusiasm for a war on Iraq well under control. There was no popular clamor for war. If the United States had never gone to war against Iraq, most Americans would hardly have cared, or even noticed. It took one man to decide for war, and to promote it, sending thousands of troops there while other nations doubted that a war was justified.

What is the status of the Bush Doctrine today? The entire case for preventive war rests on the assumption that we have accurate and reliable intelligence about the enemy's intentions and military capability—accurate and reliable enough to send our young men and women to kill and die.

But "instead of using intelligence as evidence on which to base a decision about policy," as Robin Cook, the former British foreign secretary who resigned from Tony Blair's cabinet over the war, said, "we used intelligence as the basis on which to justify a policy on which we had already settled." We note now, as some of the press recovers its manhood, the zeal with which Bush and his allies seized upon crumbs of intelligence that supported their policy—some fake, some fallacious, some flawed, some out of date or plagiarized.*

---

*There is the mystery of Mossad, the Israeli intelligence agency. Mossad has long had an exalted reputation, and its eye has long been focused on

The Bush administration thus had "not one doubt" about Saddam Hussein's weapons of mass destruction. Nor did it have any doubt about his partnership with Osama bin Laden, or about his capacity to quickly build a nuclear bomb, or about the joyous welcome as liberators that would be given our GIs. According to Philip Stephens's *Tony Blair*, Vice President Cheney told a high-ranking British official, "Once we have victory in Baghdad, all the critics will look like fools." The collapse of such confident predictions suggests that the Bush Doctrine calls for an infallibility not available to the CIA. The doctrine, observed Senator Dianne Feinstein of California, "requires a faith in the perfectibility of intelligence analysis that is simply not attainable." We can't ever know all the things we ought to know before going to war. The administration's credibility gap in Iraq finishes the Bush Doctrine of preventive war. As Senator Edward Kennedy of Massachusetts puts it, "We were tricked into a war on Iraq that has made the *real* war against terrorism harder to win and driven our reputation in the world to its lowest point in all our history."

Iraq. In 1981 Israeli planes, presumably guided by Mossad, destroyed an Iraqi nuclear reactor. Mossad had the most compelling motives to continue monitoring and penetrating the government of Saddam Hussein and far greater opportunities to do so than the CIA. Yet Mossad was evidently quite as ignorant of the true WMD situation as American intelligence. Or was it? That is the mystery. Yossi Sarid, an opposition legislator, says that Mossad knew Iraq had no WMDs but did not tell the U.S. government because Israel wanted the war to proceed—*New York Times*, March 29, 2004.

Following the attack of September 11, the Afghan war was necessary, since the Taliban refused to turn over bin Laden; but the Iraq War was the president's unilateral choice. Mr. Bush has led us into a ghastly mess—a "quagmire"—as a result of his administration's spectacular incompetence in planning for the aftermath. Americans have had little historical experience in Iraq, save for missionaries and oilmen. There were damned few Arabic speakers in State, the Pent-agon, or the CIA. Senator Richard Lugar of Indiana, the Republican chairman of the Senate Foreign Relations Com-mittee, has said with nonpartisan candor that the poor postwar planning resulted from administration assumptions that "simply were inadequate to begin with." Senator Chuck Hagel of Nebraska, another Republican, put it more starkly: the White House "did a miserable job of planning for a post-Saddam Iraq." The first bill is in—$87 billion today, more tomorrow. Like Milton's Samson in Gaza, we are eyeless in Iraq (probably in Gaza too).

A further consequence of the Bush Doctrine, little noticed by the media, is the pressure to get back into the nuclear weapons business. In 1994, Congress had passed the Spratt-Furse amendment stipulating that "it shall be the policy of the United States not to conduct research and development which could lead to the production by the United States of a new low-yield nuclear weapon." Low-yield nuclear weapons, fondly known as mini-nukes, are defined as under five kilotons.

The Bush administration, fearful that evil states might hide WMDs in hardened bunkers buried deep in the ground, called for a low-yield nuclear weapon known in the patois of the Pentagon as a Robust Nuclear Earth Penetrator. In May 2003, the Senate Armed Services Committee voted for repeal of the prohibition on mini-nuke research. Senators Feinstein and Kennedy then submitted an amendment restoring the original language. Supporters of the Feinstein-Kennedy amendment pointed out that mini-nukes were not toys, that five kilotons represented one third of the explosive power of the bomb that destroyed Hiroshima, that the activation of research on mini-nukes would run counter to U.S. anti-proliferation policy and would "release a chain of reactions across the world in nuclear testing" (Kennedy), that there was "no such thing as a 'usable nuclear weapon' "(Feinstein), and that "the United States should not follow a policy that we do not tolerate in others" (Senator Carl Levin of Michigan). Up to now, said Senator Byron Dorgan of South Dakota, "American policy has been to have nuclear weapons to prevent nuclear weapons from ever being used. . . . Now we have people who see them as any other weapon. They talk about using them, and they are suggesting we might need to use them first. . . . What kind of a signal do we send to other countries?" Low-yield weapons, Senator Joseph Biden of Delaware said, "blur the traditional firewall between nuclear and conventional war."

Nevertheless, the Feinstein-Kennedy amendment was tabled by a vote of 51 to 43. The House meanwhile eliminated mini-nuke research, but on September 16, 2003, the Senate defeated a revived Feinstein-Kennedy amendment. Reopening the nuclear door in a context of preventive war may have the gravest possible consequences for the human race.

It is doubtful that President Bush could once again rally a "coalition of the willing" in a preventive war against Iran or North Korea. The world believed President Kennedy in the grim days of the Cuban missile crisis. After the presidential case for a war on Iraq, no one can accept the word of the U.S. government on anything. The Bush Doctrine is already obsolete.

There are longer-range objections, too. "It is not in the American national interest," observes Henry Kissinger, "to establish preemption as a universal principle available to every nation." But to reserve that principle to the United States alone is to make our nation the world's judge, jury, and executioner. However virtuous some Americans may feel in assigning this triple role to an American president, less powerful nations are likely to hate us for it.

The recent survey by the German Marshall Fund, for example, reports an astonishing shift in European opinion of the United States. The majority of Europeans expressed strong disapproval of U.S. foreign policy, with Italians and Germans increasing their disapproval by more than twenty points over a similar survey in 2003. After September 11, *Le Monde* of Paris, not notably pro-American, declared: "*Nous Sommes Tous Américains.*" After the Iraq War, Jean Daniel, in the past pro-American, declared in *Le Nouvel Observateur*: "*Nous Ne Sommes Pas Tous Américains.*" The Bush administration, following the counsel of Machiavelli—"far safer to be feared than loved"—dismisses world opinion as a matter for wimps.

They forget the wimps who fought the American

Revolution and established the new republic. "An attention to the judgment of other nations is important to every government for two reasons," declared the 63rd *Federalist*:

> The one is, that, independently of the merits of any particular plan or measure, it is desirable, on various accounts, that it should appear to other nations as the offspring of a wise and honorable policy; the second is, that in doubtful cases, particularly where the national councils may be warped by some strong passion or momentary interest, the presumed or known opinion of the impartial world may be the best guide that can be followed.

Moreover, by encouraging self-righteousness and arrogance, the triple role is bound to corrupt our own country. As John Quincy Adams, perhaps our greatest secretary of state, said on July 4, 1821, "Wherever the standard of freedom and independence has been or shall be unfurled, there will [America's] heart, her benedictions and her prayers be. But she goes not abroad in search of monsters to destroy." Once embroiled in foreign wars of interest and intrigue, Adams predicted,

> the fundamental maxims of her policy would insensibly change from liberty to force. . . . She might become the dictatress of the world: she would no longer be the ruler of her own spirit.

The atmospherics of the Bush presidency, the militant unilateralism, the passion for military supremacy, the scorn for international law and institutions, the contempt for due process, the conviction of American moral superiority over lesser breeds—all this ends at Abu Ghraib and fulfills Adams's prediction.

The triple role as judge, jury, executioner resurrects the imperial presidency. Again there are warnings from the American past. On February 15, 1848, during the war with Mexico, a young Illinois congressman sent a letter to his law partner pointing out the constitutional and practical flaws in what we now call the Bush Doctrine. "Allow the President to invade a neighboring nation whenever he shall deem it necessary to repel an invasion," Abraham Lincoln wrote William H. Herndon,

> and you allow him to do so *whenever he may choose to say* he deems it necessary for such purpose, and you allow him to make war at pleasure. . . . If today he should choose to say he thinks it necessary to invade Canada to prevent the British from invading us, how could you stop him? You may say to him, "I see no probability of the British invading us"; but he will say to you, "Be silent: I see it, if you don't."

The Philadelphia convention, Lincoln said, had "resolved to so frame the Constitution that *no one man* should hold the power of bringing this oppression upon us."

The American president as the world's self-appointed judge, jury, and executioner?—the road that led straight to Abu Ghraib. Never in American history has the United States been so unpopular abroad, so regarded with hostility, so distrusted, feared, hated. There is irony here. After 9/11, a wave of worldwide sympathy engulfed America. Three years later, the Bush Doctrine had converted that warm sympathy into cold hate. Margaret Tutwiler, a veteran Republican operative placed in charge of public diplomacy at the State Department, told a House appropriations subcommittee in February 2004— two months before the Abu Ghraib photos delivered the coup de grâce to America's moral reputation—that America's standing abroad had so deteriorated that "it will take years of hard, focused work" to repair it. Or a regime change in Washington?

Let us recall the warning against hubris issued by President John F. Kennedy in November 1961. "We must face the fact," President Kennedy said,

> that the United States is neither omnipotent or omniscient—that we are only 6 percent of the world's population—that we cannot impose our will upon the other 94 percent of mankind—that we cannot right every wrong or reverse each adversity—and that therefore there cannot be an American solution to every world problem.

CHAPTER 3

THE IMPERIAL PRESIDENCY REDUX

M y book *The Imperial Presidency* was written in the latter days, hectic and ominous, of the presidency of Richard M. Nixon. The American Constitution, the book argued, envisages a strong presidency within an equally strong system of accountability. When the constitutional balance is upset in favor of presidential power and at the expense of presidential accountability, the presidency can be said to become imperial.

The perennial threat to the constitutional balance, I suggested, arises in the field of foreign affairs. Confronted by presidential initiatives in domestic policy, the countervailing branches of the national government—the legislative and the judiciary—have ample confidence in their own information and judgment. In this area they do not hesitate to challenge what they deem executive pretensions, nor do they lightly surrender power to the presidency. The media and public opinion, those extraconstitutional checks on the abuse of executive power, are similarly assured in dealing with domestic policy.

But confronted by presidential initiatives in foreign affairs, Congress and the courts, along with the press and the citizenry too, often lack confidence in their own information and judgment and are likely to be intimidated by executive authority. The inclination in foreign policy is to let the president have the responsibility and the power—a renunciation that results from congressional pusillanimity as well as from presidential rapacity. The more acute the crisis, the more power flows to the president.

"It is chiefly in its foreign relations," Alexis de Tocqueville noted early on, "that the executive power of a nation finds occasion to exert its skill and its strength. If the existence of the American Union were perpetually threatened, if its chief interests were in daily connection with those of other powerful nations, the executive would assume an increased importance." But the young republic Tocqueville visited in the 1830s had lived, at least since the War of 1812, in happy isolation from world power struggles. So "the President of the United States," Tocqueville observed, "possesses almost royal prerogatives which he has no opportunity of exercising."

By the twentieth century the United States itself had become a world power, its interests in daily connection with those of other powers; and the half century from Pearl Harbor to the breakup of the Soviet Union was experienced as a time of perpetual threat to the American Union. The chronic international crisis known as the Cold War at last gave presidents the opportunity for sustained exercise of those almost royal prerogatives. What began as emergency powers temporarily confided to presidents soon hardened into authority claimed by presidents as constitutionally inherent in the presidential office: thus the imperial presidency.

The rise of the imperial presidency ran against the original intent of the framers of the Constitution. With the warmaking propensities of absolute monarchs in mind, the framers took care to assign the vital foreign policy powers exclusively to Congress. Article I gave Congress not only the appropriations power—itself a potent instrument of control—but also the power to declare war, to raise and support armies, to provide and maintain a navy, to regulate commerce, and to grant letters of "marque and reprisal." This last provision represented the eighteenth-century equivalent of retaliatory strikes and empowered Congress to authorize limited as well as general war.

Even Alexander Hamilton, the Constitutional Convention's foremost proponent of executive energy, endorsed this allocation of powers. "The history of human conduct," he wrote in *Federalist 75*, "does not warrant that exalted opinion of human virtue which would make it wise to commit interests of so delicate and momentous a kind, as those which concern its intercourse with the rest of the world, to the sole disposal of . . . a President of the United States." What seemed at stake was not only the wisdom of the policy but the freedom of the people. "Perhaps it is a universal truth," said James Madison, "that the loss of liberty at home is to be charged to provisions against danger, real or pretended, from abroad."

The specific grants of authority to the executive in foreign policy were trivial compared with the authority specifically granted to Congress. The presidency was only given the power of receiving and appointing ambassadors and, by implication, of serving as the channel of communications to foreign states. As commander in chief, the president was given the power to direct the armed forces when war was authorized by Congress and, by implication, the power to repel sudden attacks when Congress was not in session. However, Article II vested broad executive power in the presidency. And, as *Federalist 64* and *75* emphasized, the structural advantages of the presidency—unity, decision, secrecy, dispatch, stability of purpose, special sources of information—made the executive the prime agent in dealings with foreign affairs.

Those structural advantages worked against the framers' original intent. "It is of the nature of war," Hamilton wrote in *Federalist 8*, "to increase the executive at the expense of the legislative authority." The pattern of presidential aggrandizement under the spur of international crisis was visible from the start. In opposition, Thomas Jefferson had been the apostle of strict construction and the foe of executive initiative. But viewing problems from the White House, he sent a naval squadron to the Mediterranean under secret orders to fight pirates in the Barbary War, applied for congressional sanction six months later, then misled Congress as to the nature of his orders. He unilaterally authorized the seizure of armed vessels in waters extending to the Gulf Stream, engaged in rearmament without congressional appropriations, withheld information from Congress, and invoked John Locke's doc-

trine of emergency prerogative—the law of self-preservation—
to justify action beyond congressional authorization.

Early presidents did not hesitate to engage in what later
generations called "covert operations" against foreign states
and to do so without congressional knowledge. James Madison
sent Joel K. Poinsett as a secret agent to Latin America and
winked at his clandestine revolutionary adventures in
Argentina and Chile; the secretary of state removed Poinsett's
dispatches from State Department files lest Congress request
them. Both Madison and James Monroe used covert action
to facilitate the annexation of Florida.

Presidential adventurism in the early republic differed in
salient respects, however, from the imperial presidency. As
Abraham D. Sofaer shows in his magisterial work, *War, Foreign
Affairs, and Constitutional Power: The Origins* (1976), early presidents deliberately selected venturesome agents, deliberately
kept their missions secret, deliberately gave them vague
instructions, deliberately failed either to approve or to disapprove their constitutionally questionable plans, and deliberately denied Congress the information to determine whether
aggressive acts were authorized—all precisely because the
presidents wanted their men in the field to do things they
knew lay beyond their constitutional right to command. "At
no time," Sofaer writes of the early period, "did the executive
claim 'inherent' power to initiate military actions."

The early presidents thus usurped power, and usurpation
creates no constitutional precedents. It is the assertion of
inherent powers that defines the imperial presidency and creates precedents for the future. The contrast in constitutional

claims between the emergency policies of Abraham Lincoln and Franklin D. Roosevelt and those of post–Second World War presidents illustrates the distinction.

Both Lincoln and Roosevelt were well aware what the Constitution said about the warmaking power. In 1848, Lincoln called the Mexican War illegal and unconstitutional because it was unilaterally provoked, so he believed, by President James K. Polk. The founding fathers at Philadelphia, Lincoln said, had "resolved to so frame the Constitution that *no one man* should hold power of bringing this oppression [war] upon us." Similarly Roosevelt in 1940, promising supplies to a French government under Nazi assault, carefully added: "These statements carry with them no implication of military commitments. Only Congress can make such commitments."

Yet after the attack on Fort Sumter in 1861, Lincoln, on his own, without congressional authorization, assembled the militia, enlarged the Army and Navy beyond their authorized strength, called out volunteers for three years' service, spent unappropriated public funds, suspended habeas corpus, arrested persons "represented" as involved in "disloyal" practices, and instituted a naval blockade of the rebel states. Similarly in 1941, when German submarine warfare threatened to sever the lifeline of supplies to Britain, Roosevelt, on his own, without congressional authorization, dispatched troops to Iceland, instituted a convoy system, issued a "shoot-on-sight" order to the U.S. Navy, and launched an undeclared war in the North Atlantic.

But neither president based his action on claims of inherent power. His emergency measures, Lincoln told Congress when he finally convoked a special session, "whether strictly legal or not, were ventured upon under what appeared to be a popular demand and a public necessity; trusting then as now that Congress would readily ratify them." Roosevelt, like Lincoln, relied on his sense of popular demand and public necessity. The passage of the Lend-Lease Act (1941) after uninhibited public and congressional debate had aligned the United States with Great Britain in the European war. If Congress voted arms to Britain as national policy, then, inferentially, national policy was to make sure the arms got to Britain. Roosevelt added a murky proclamation of "unlimited national emergency." But, like Lincoln, he made no claims of inherent power to do what he believed necessary to save the nation.

Both Lincoln and Roosevelt undertook acts they knew to be beyond the Constitution. Both did so in times of transcendent crisis when the life of the nation seemed truly at stake. Both acted, knowingly or not, on Locke's doctrine of emergency prerogative, trusting that Congress would eventually approve their actions. Both men understood and affirmed that emergency prerogative must expire with the emergency. "The Executive power itself," said Lincoln, "would be greatly diminished by the cessation of actual war." "When the war is won," said Roosevelt, "the powers under which I act automatically revert to the people—to whom they belong." Neither Lincoln nor Roosevelt claimed an inherent and routine presidential right to do what they did. That claim, the essence of the imperial presidency, was a product of the second half of the twentieth century.

The rarety of international crisis delayed the emergence of the imperial presidency. For, while war increased presidential power, peace brought a reaction against executive excess. The Civil War, Henry Adams wrote, "for the time obliterated the Constitution." It produced what Benjamin R. Curtis, one of the two dissenting justices in *Dred Scott v. Sanford* (1857), charged was "a military despotism." But once the crisis ended, the other two branches of government lost no time in reasserting their constitutional powers. A year after Appomattox, the Supreme Court held in *ex parte Milligan* (1866) that Lincoln's prosecution of a proslavery conspirator under martial law behind the lines violated the Constitution. In another two years, Lincoln's successor in the White House found himself at the bar of impeachment. The republic entered the era characterized by Woodrow Wilson as one of "congressional government."

Wilson himself, writing a new preface to *Congressional Government* after the Spanish-American War, remarked on "the greatly increased power . . . given the President by the plunge into international politics." When foreign policy became the nation's dominant concern, Wilson said, the executive "must of necessity be its guide: must utter every initial judgment, take every first step of action, supply the information upon which it is to act, suggest and in large measure control its conduct." As president during the First World War, Wilson acted on his own model.

But once again the return of peace shrank presidential power, as the Senate quickly showed by rejecting the Treaty of Versailles. In the next decade Roosevelt, a persuasive

domestic president, could not prevent Congress from imposing rigid neutrality legislation that put American foreign policy in a straitjacket while Germany and Japan ran amok in
Europe and Asia.

The end of the Second World War brought the usual
diminution of presidential power. A year after Roosevelt's
death, his successor was so unpopular that voters said "To err
is Truman" and elected a Republican Congress. The next year
Congress gained posthumous revenge against the powerful
wartime president by proposing what became the Twenty-
Second Amendment, thereby limiting all future presidents to
two terms.

But this time the diminution was brief. The Cold War, by
generating a climate of sustained and indefinite crisis, aborted
the customary reversion of power to the coordinate branches.
The most visible sign of growing executive imperialism was
the transfer of the power to go to war from Congress to the
presidency. Ten years after Roosevelt told France that only
Congress could make military commitments, President
Harry S. Truman, confronted by the North Korean invasion
of South Korea, sent American forces to war on his own.

Historically, Congress had preserved the rough balance of
the Constitution because it retained three vital powers: the
warmaking power; the power of the purse; and the power of
oversight and investigation. In 1950 it relinquished the warmaking power. Truman fought in Korea, Lyndon B. Johnson
in Vietnam, and Richard M. Nixon in Cambodia without
believing that their dispatch of troops into combat required
explicit congressional authorization (Congress provided

ambiguous authorization in the case of Vietnam through the 1964 Gulf of Tonkin resolution). In 1969–74, the Nixon administration tried systematically and, until the Watergate affair, successfully to restrict the other two powers: countering the power of the purse by the doctrine of the unlimited impoundment of appropriated funds and countering the power of oversight and investigation by the doctrine of unreviewable "executive privilege" (a novel term, first used officially in 1958) and the extension of the executive secrecy system. Had Nixon succeeded in imposing these doctrines on top of his amplified claims for the presidential warmaking power, he would have gravely weakened Congress as a serious partner in the constitutional order.

Nixon carried the imperial presidency still further by using against his political opponents at home—"enemies," he called them—powers that the presidency had accumulated to save the republic from foreign foes. Invoking national security as an all-purpose justification, Nixon and his attorney general, John Mitchell, set up a secret White House posse to burgle offices, forge historical documents, and wiretap officials, embassies, newspapermen, and "enemies." "When the President does it," Nixon claimed in 1977, "that means that it is not illegal." Congress eventually roused itself. Articles of impeachment charged Nixon with acting "in a manner contrary to his trust as President and subversive of constitutional government," and Nixon resigned rather than be impeached and face a trial. Mitchell was later found guilty of perjury, conspiracy, and obstruction of justice, and served a prison term.

The imperial presidency reached a twentieth-century climax with Nixon. The post–Watergate reaction cut back on presidential excesses. None of Nixon's successors, for example, used emergency powers against political opponents. The presidency of Jimmy Carter even led to concerns about the impotence of the office. "We have not an imperial presidency," former President Gerald Ford said in 1980, "but an imperiled presidency." But such lamentations were soon refuted when Ronald Reagan showed that a president with only a vague understanding of issues could still dominate the government and lead the country.

Nor did the reaction constrain executive assumption of the warmaking power. Reagan in the case of Grenada and George H. W. Bush in the cases of Panama and Iraq insisted on what Bush called "the President's constitutional authority to use the armed forces to defend vital U.S. interests." In the Iraq case, Congress rescued Bush from a constitutional conflict by voting to authorize the first Gulf War. However, the end of the Cold War materially weakened arguments for the imperial presidency.

The farewell to the Cold War and, for a moment, to international crisis meant the customary setback for presidential power. The presidency was evidently in decline once again. In August 1998, I wrote an Op Ed piece for the *New York Times* entitled "So Much for the Imperial Presidency." These were the latter days, also hectic and ominous, of the beleaguered presidency of Bill Clinton—"a presidency," I wrote, "harried and enfeebled by an obsessed special prosecutor."

Fellow presidential scholars shared in obituaries for the

imperial presidency. "The U.S. presidency," wrote Richard E. Neustadt, "has been progressively weakened over the past three decades to the point where it is probably weaker today than at almost any time in the preceding century." Michael Beschloss, titling his column "The End of the Imperial Presidency," portrayed George W. Bush as "the first truly post-imperial president."

We presidential scholars reckoned without Osama bin Laden, who of course has resurrected the imperial presidency. Much of the impact of resurgent presidential power on American liberties is dependent on the presidential choice of attorney general. After the First World War, a sick and distracted Woodrow Wilson permitted his attorney general, A. Mitchell Palmer, the Fighting Quaker (aka the Quaking Fighter), to run wild in fomenting a Red Scare series of raids and mass arrests. During the Second World War Franklin D. Roosevelt's selection as attorney general was Francis Biddle, a strong civil libertarian. The result was a pretty good wartime record on individual rights (with, of course, the notable exception of the internment of Japanese-Americans, which Biddle opposed). During the Cold War, John Mitchell, Nixon's attorney general, happily connived with his boss at dirty tricks and became the first attorney general to go to jail.

The situation in Washington today? President Bush's attorney general, John Ashcroft, a former senator, a politician of the hard right, and a religious zealot, is on the model of A. Mitchell Palmer rather than of Francis Biddle. According to Steven Brill, the legal critic, "even some of his own deputies at Justice were surprised by how uninterested he was in the niceties of the law. One veteran staffer recalls that . . . he had never once heard Ashcroft cite a legal case and had watched him blanch when someone in the room cited a case, as if that person was discourteously speaking another language." A righteous fellow, a communicant of an evangelical sect that disapproves of drinking, dancing, going to movies, and gazing at nude statues, Ashcroft puts one in mind of Mr. Dooley's definition of a fanatic—someone who "does what he thinks th' Lord wud do if He only knew th' facts in th' case."

John Ashcroft is given to early morning prayer meetings held in his office. When he was elected to the Senate, according to Judy Bachrach's sketch in *Vanity Fair* (February 2004), friends anointed his head with oil in the style of the ancient kings of Israel, although in this case it was Crisco oil from the kitchen. Ashcroft, a man of pious poses, lacked when young a stern view of his patriotic duty. During the Vietnam War, he sought and received seven deferments, including an occupational deferment for teaching business law to undergraduates at a Missouri college, "an assignment," according to the *New Republic*, "he lined up with the help of a family friend." Since Ashcroft was presumably in favor of the Vietnam War, he joins the serried ranks of chickenhawks that adorn the second Bush presidency. In Vice President Cheney's felicitous phrase, the Bush chickenhawks had "other priorities" than military service in Vietnam.

Ashcroft's chosen national security vehicle is the 342-page USA Patriot Act, rushed to passage without hearings or committee reports forty-five days after 9/11 by a vote of 357 to 66 in the House and 98 to 1 in the Senate. All honor to Russ

Feingold of Wisconsin, the single Senate holdout! The Patriot Act increases the discretionary power of federal agents to collect information about individuals, to search their homes, to inspect their reading habits and their Internet queries, to view their credit reports, to conduct wiretaps without warrants and overhear lawyer-client telephone conversations without court orders, to reduce judicial supervision, and to spy on domestic organizations and advocacy groups. In a report to Congress, the Department of Justice said that federal agents had conducted hundreds of bugging and surveillance operations and visited numerous libraries and mosques.

The FBI is part of Attorney General Ashcroft's domain. On Christmas Eve 2003, the FBI sent a zany bulletin to eighteen thousand police organizations warning against people carrying almanacs. There is nothing more innocent, one would think, than to give next year's *World Almanac* for Christmas. But, according to the FBI, terrorists might use the almanacs "to assist with target selection and preoperational planning." Citizens are asked to report almanac carriers to the local U.S. Joint Terrorism Task Force.

The Patriot Act alarmed libertarians on the right, like William Safire of the *New York Times*, as well as the American Civil Liberties Union crowd on the left. In a case before the Supreme Court, the Cato Institute, a rightist libertarian think tank, filed a brief arguing that "if the government determines that an American citizen must be deprived of his liberty because he poses a threat to public safety, it must be prepared to defend that assessment in a court of law." Bob Barr of Georgia, the dogged impeacher of Bill Clinton, joined

Grover Norquist and David Keene, veteran right-wing leaders, in an ACLU rally protesting the Patriot Act. As Norquist said, "Some day Hillary Clinton's going to be attorney general, and I hope conservatives keep that in mind."

The temper of the administration as shown by its wish lists is even more alarming. In January 2003, there fell into the hands of Charles Lewis, head of the invaluable Center for Public Integrity, an eighty-page draft of a presumed Patriot Act II. The proposed amendments would authorize secret arrests, would relax restrictions on wiretapping, would facilitate the stripping of citizenship, and would in general limit the role of judicial oversight and give the Department of Justice looser standards to brand individuals and groups as terrorist suspects. The libertarian, left-wing coalition bridled; thus far there has been no Patriot II.

The Bush Pentagon meanwhile hauled out of oblivion a discredited official, John Poindexter, convicted of five felony counts of lying to Congress about the Iran-Contra affair (the verdict was reversed on a technicality). Poindexter headed a so-called Total Information Awareness (TIA) project, an electronic databank based on federal, state, local, and commercial records, credit card transactions, telephone calls, travel reservations, and so on. This Orwellian concept was too much even for Republicans, and TIA was stopped in its tracks.

The plight of the 660 men (and boys) picked up in Afghanistan after 9/11 and transported to Guantánamo Bay, the American base in Cuba, excited little interest in the United States, but a good deal abroad, especially in Great Britain. The U.S. government declined to grant al-Qaeda jihadists prisoner-of-war status for plausible reasons—there was no organized state behind them. Also government lawyers denied that Guantánamo, held under lease, was sovereign U.S. soil; so U.S. law did not apply. The detainees were kept in ignorance of the charges against them and were denied access to counsel, to hearings, and to their families. They existed in legal limbo.

It is difficult to find serious security reasons for presidential suspension of due process. Some detainees were unquestionably al-Qaeda or Taliban thugs, fanatics, and killers; others may have been innocent bystanders, snatched up by accident in random sweeps. The detainees included octogenarians and teenagers. They were collectively defined as "unlawful enemy combatants," a classification unknown to international law. They were subject to intensive regimens of day-and-night interrogation. A "senior defense official" told the *New York Times* that detainees would be held for many years, perhaps indefinitely. Some among them have attempted suicide.

"If the government denies that foreign nationals have rights," argued one brief submitted to the Supreme Court, "then by confining them at Guantánamo, it is engaged not in legal detention, but in a lawless exercise of legal force." The brief was signed by eight former officials, including two secretaries of the Navy. "The question," said Lord Steyn, a judge on Britain's highest court, "is whether the quality of justice envisaged for the prisoners at Guantánamo Bay complies with the minimum international standards for the conduct of fair trials. The answer can be given quite shortly. It is a resounding 'No.'" After pleas from Tony Blair, five British prisoners were released, some of whom then claimed to the London press that they had been beaten by American guards. "Three of the other released British detainees," reported *The Economist*, "confirm Mr. Al-Harith's claim of frequent physical abuse and beating. They had each been subject to more than 200 interrogations lasting up to 12 hours." American officials in turn denied the stories. No photographs have thus far emerged as in Abu Ghraib, and the conflict in testimony invites a congressional investigation.

The second Bush presidency is the most secretive administration since Nixon. Indeed, John W. Dean, who knew the Nixon White House well, writes that "George W. Bush and Richard B. Cheney have created the most secretive presidency of my lifetime. Their secrecy is far worse than during Watergate." Dean should have added Ashcroft to his list of secrecy addicts.

In 1966, Congress had passed the Freedom of Information Act based on the proposition that disclosure should be the rule, not the exception, and that the burden should be on government to justify the withholding of records. This was a most beneficial law until Ashcroft got hold of it. Rejecting the spirit of the law, the attorney general advised federal officials that when they "decide to withhold records, in whole or in part, you can be assured that the Department of Justice will defend your decisions."

Following the argument over who owned Richard Nixon's papers, Congress had passed in 1978 the Presidential Records Act based on the proposition that White House records belonged to the American people and should be made available within a dozen years. A president could restrict access to six enumerated categories, ranging from national security papers to medical files. But the 1978 act breathed the post-Watergate spirit of open government.

One of President Bush's early actions was to alter the methodology and to narrow the scope of the Presidential Records Act, and to do so—i.e., amend a congressional statute—by executive order. His Executive Order 13223 gave sitting presidents the right to cancel the release of papers from a previous administration, even though the previous administration had approved their release. This gave rise to the uneasy suspicion that the people behind Executive Order 13223 had secrets they wished to hide from Congress and the media. President Bush's attack on the Presidential Records Act enraged historians, political scientists, archivists, and journalists, and the American Historical Association organized a lawsuit. In Congress the executive order offended Republicans as well as Democrats, and in October 2002 the House Government Reform Committee unanimously voted to overturn it. The White House moved quickly to suppress the rebellion.

The most famous case involving official secrecy was the disclosure by Daniel Ellsberg of the highly classified Pentagon Papers during the Nixon presidency. It fell to a conscientious solicitor general, Erwin Griswold, former dean of the Harvard Law School, to make the case for the prosecution. Griswold asked three high-level security officials to pick out items that could conceivably constitute threats to the security of the republic. They came up with around forty items. Most

Griswold dismissed as trivial, thereby reducing the list to eleven items he thought faintly arguable.

The eleven did not impress the Supreme Court, and the Pentagon Papers were published in their entirety. The republic survived. The threats to national security? As Griswold observed eighteen years later, "I have never seen a trace of a threat to the national security from the publication. Indeed, I have never seen it even suggested that there was such an actual threat. . . . It quickly becomes apparent to any person who has considerable experience with classified material that there is massive overclassification and that the principal concern of the classifiers is not with national security, but rather with governmental embarrassment of one sort or another."

Imperial suggests empire, and the status of the United States as the world's unchallengeable superpower headed by an imperial presidency rouses speculation over the future and fate of the American Empire. Comparisons are often made to the Roman Empire and to the modern British and French empires. Is the American Empire a fitting successor?

Now Americans, unlike Romans, Britons, and the French, are not colonizers of remote and exotic places. We peopled the vacant spaces, as we whites deemed them, in continental expansion from sea to shining sea, but we did not send away our youngest sons to man the outposts of empire. Britain really created a British world in India and Africa, as the French did in equatorial Africa and Indochina. Americans, wrote James Bryce in 1888, "have none of the earth-hunger which burns in the great nations of Europe."

Some of our political leaders did. Jefferson thought Cuba

"the most interesting addition which could ever be made to our system of States" and told John C. Calhoun in 1820 that the United States "ought, at the first possible opportunity, to take Cuba." John Quincy Adams agreed, considering the annexation of Cuba "indispensable to the continuance and integrity of the Union itself," and supposing Cuba would inexorably fall to the United States by the law of political gravitation.

As for Canada, John Quincy Adams held "our proper domain to be the continent of North America." "That the whole continent of North America and all its adjacent islands," said Henry Adams, JQ's grandson, in 1869, "must at last fall under the control of the United States is a conviction absolutely ingrained in our people." "Long ere the second centennial arrives," Walt Whitman wrote in *Democratic Vistas* (1871), "there will be some forty to fifty great States, among them Canada and Cuba." As late as 1895, Henry Cabot Lodge declared, "From the Rio Grande to the Arctic Ocean there would be but one flag and one country."

These things, so authoritatively predicted, never came to pass. The American people were not much interested in empire. The United States has not annexed Cuba or Canada. There is no likelihood that we ever will. Texas waited outside the Union for a decade as an independent republic and then entered only through presidential sleight-of-hand, John Tyler procuring admission by joint resolution after the U.S. Senate had rejected a treaty of annexation. The movement during the Mexican War to take "all Mexico" failed. President Polk even feared that Congress would turn against the war and that he would lose California and New Mexico. The Ostend Manifesto was disclaimed, and the filibusters of the 1850s were repudiated.

After the Civil War, Secretary of State William H. Seward's ambitious expansionist program got nowhere, except for the flyspeck of Midway and for Alaska, which Russia wanted to get rid of and which Congress reluctantly accepted after members were bribed, perhaps by the Russian minister. The Senate rejected the Hawaiian reciprocity treaty, the purchase of the Virgin Islands from Denmark, the annexation of Santo Domingo, and the annexation of Samoa. It took half a century of argument before we annexed Hawaii, and this might not have taken place had it not been for the Spanish-American War. Even with that war, we still did not annex Cuba. We did annex the Philippines, but the number of Americans who lived out their lives in the archipelago was negligible, and we set the islands free forty years later. The imperial dream has encountered consistent indifference and recurrent resistance through American history. The record hardly sustains the thesis of a people red hot for empire.

Then there is the question of control. "The term 'empire,'" writes Professor G. John Ikenberry, summing up the common understanding, "refers to the political control by a dominant country of the domestic and foreign policies of weaker countries." Rome, London, Paris, despite slow and awkward lines of communication, really ruled their empires. Today, communication is instantaneous; but, despite the speed of contact, Washington, far from ruling an empire in the old sense, becomes the prisoner of its dependent states.

This was the case with South Vietnam in the 1960s, and it has been the case ever since with Israel. Governments in Saigon forty years ago and in Tel Aviv today have been sure that the United States would not pull out, or even significantly reduce American aid. They therefore were enabled to defy American commands and demands with impunity. Pakistan, Taiwan, Egypt, South Korea, the Philippines are similarly unimpressed, evasive, or defiant. For all our superhuman military strength, we cannot get our Latin American neighbors, or even the tiny Caribbean islands, to do our bidding. Americans are simply not competent imperialists, as demonstrated in Iraq in 2005. The so-called American Empire is in fact a feeble imitation of the Roman, British, and French empires.

And yet the American presidency has come to see itself in messianic terms as the appointed savior of a world whose unpredictable dangers call for rapid and incessant deployment of men, arms, and decisions behind a wall of secrecy. This view seems hard to reconcile with the American Constitution. The impact of 9/11 and of the overhanging terrorist threat gives more power than ever to the imperial presidency and places the separation of powers ordained by the Constitution under unprecedented, and at times unbearable, strain.

But superhuman military power cannot solve everything, even if American presidents were free to use such power without constraints, as they are not. As a world empire, the United States is undone by its own domestic politics and its own humane, pluralistic, and tolerant ideals. The premises of our national existence undermine our imperial aspirations. So the imperial presidency redux is likely to continue messing things up, as we are doing so successfully in Iraq, the needless war. Then democracy's singular virtue—its capacity for self-correction—will one day swing into action.

CHAPTER 4

PATRIOTISM AND DISSENT IN WARTIME

W ar, as we have seen, nourishes the imperial presidency. The suspension of criticism and dissent is acceptable when the life of the nation is under mortal threat. And we are surely under mortal threat these days from international terrorism.

Many Americans now feel a personal vulnerability they have never felt before. The Second World War was a far more menacing conflict with far more dangerous foes, but Americans behind the lines were not in any sort of danger as they went about their daily business. They think they are today. "Two years after the 9/11 terrorist attacks," reports the Pew Research Center, "fully three-quarters of Americans saw the world as a more dangerous place than a decade ago." Terrorism, striking from the shadows, gives a new and frightening dimension to life—a dimension intensified by Washington's color-coded exploitation of the politics of fear.

In this unprecedented national mood of personal vulnerability, the idea spreads that, when deadly danger threatens, the time has come for patriotic Americans to cease debate and rally round the flag, giving the president total support as the single voice of a united nation. "What have we elected him for," observes James Bowman in Hilton Kramer's right-wing *New Criterion* (October 2002), "if we are to act as if we expected our views to be treated as being of equal weight with his?"

All this raises a couple of questions—questions that history might help us answer. The first question is whether a democratic people has a moral obligation to terminate dissent when the nation is at war. And the second question is whether, as a factual matter, our ancestors abstained from dissent when their governments took them into war. These two questions presuppose a third: What is the true nature of patriotism anyway?

Of course, America was born in dissent. "We have been told that it is unpatriotic to criticize public action," said Woodrow Wilson. "Well, if it is, then there is a deep disgrace resting upon the origins of this nation. This nation originated in the sharpest sort of criticism of public policy. . . . We have forgotten the very principle of our origin if we have forgotten how to object, how to resist, how to agitate, how to pull down and build up."

Nor does going to war change the originating principle (though in Wilson's case, it lamentably did). Going to war does not abrogate the freedoms of conscience, thought, and speech. "The Constitution of the United States," the Supreme Court declared in *ex parte Milligan*, "is a law for rulers and people, equally in war and in peace." War does not nullify the Bill of Rights. Even when the republic faces mortal dangers, the First Amendment is still in the Constitution.

When I think of the American flag, I think of Flag Day in 1943. On that day, June 14, in the midst of a great and terrible war, the Supreme Court clarified the meaning of the flag as a symbol of patriotism.

To achieve this clarification, the Court had to overrule itself. In 1940, before the United States entered the Second World War, the Court had upheld compulsory flag salutes and compulsory pledges of allegiance for students in public schools. "National unity," the Court declared in *Minersville School District v. Gobitis*, "is the basis of national security." On that ground, a Pennsylvania school board had a perfect right to expel kids who refused to recite the pledge of allegiance and refused to salute the flag. The Gobitis children were guilty even though as Jehovah's Witnesses they were brought up to believe that the flag salute and the pledge of allegiance violated the Second Commandment.

The *Gobitis* decision led to widespread persecution of Jehovah's Witnesses. Mobs of self-appointed "patriots" harassed Witnesses, beat them up, and punished one unfortunate fellow by castration. Then, three years later, in the case of *West Virginia State Board of Education v. Barnette*, the Supreme Court reversed *Gobitis*, by a 6–3 vote. This time the Court held that laws compelling students in public schools to salute the flag and to recite the pledge of allegiance were unconstitutional.

The Court spoke through Justice Robert H. Jackson, next to Oliver Wendell Holmes the best writer on the Court in the twentieth century. Jackson rested the decision on the First Amendment. Saluting the flag and pledging allegiance, Jackson said, were forms of speech. To require people to do these things violated their constitutional right to freedom of speech.

"If there is any fixed star in our constitutional constellation," Justice Jackson said, "it is that no official, high or petty, can prescribe what shall be orthodox in politics, nationalism, religion, or other matters of opinion or force citizens to confess by word or act their faith therein."

This decision, as noted, was handed down on Flag Day 1943. Young Americans were fighting and dying for the American flag on many fronts around the planet. But the high Court's veto of compulsory flag salutes and compulsory pledges of allegiance was generally applauded. Most Americans in 1943 thought the decision was a pretty good statement of what we were fighting for.

The flag thus incorporates the First Amendment. But today, in another national emergency, officials seek to narrow the meaning of the flag, to identify the flag with the president and his war. At the time of the *Barnette* case, the attorney general for the United States, Francis Biddle, was a strong civil libertarian. Sixty years later, a religious zealot occupies Biddle's office.

Let us not surrender the flag to Attorney General Ashcroft. As Woodrow Wilson said, there is much history written upon the folds of the American flag. "If you will teach the children what the flag stands for, I am willing that they should go on both knees to it. But they will get up with opinions of their own; they will not get up with the opinions which happen to be the opinions of those who are instructing them. They will get up critical." People who protest the war against Iraq have as much right to rally round the flag as hyperpatriots cheering on the war.

The role of dissent in the run-up to war is crucial in a democracy. Of all the decisions a free people must face, questions of war and peace are the most solemn. Before sending young Americans to kill and die in foreign lands, a democracy has a sacred obligation to permit full and searching discussion of the issues at stake. There is no obligation to bow down before an imperial presidency. The views of the American people should indeed have equal weight with those of the fellow they send to the White House.

Nor does the congressional authorization of the war change the situation. As Theodore Roosevelt—no greater hyperpatriot, he—said in 1918 during the First World War, "To announce that there must be no criticism of the president, or that we are to stand by the president, right or wrong, is not only unpatriotic and servile, but is morally treasonable to the American public."

During the Second World War, within a fortnight after the attack on Pearl Harbor brought us into the war, Senator Robert A. Taft of Ohio took the same line. Senator Taft, a perennial candidate for the Republican presidential nomination, was an influential and much-revered Republican leader. "I believe," Taft said, there can be no doubt that criticism in time of war is essential to the maintenance of any kind of democratic government. . . . Too many people desire to suppress criticism simply because they think it will give some comfort to the enemy. . . . If that comfort makes the enemy feel better for a few moments, they are welcome to it as far as I am concerned, because the maintenance of the right of criticism in the long run will do the country maintaining it a great deal more good than it will do the enemy, and it will prevent mistakes which might otherwise occur.

Bob Taft was everlastingly right. Presidents are never infallible. They will not benefit from the cessation of dissent. They may even pick up a good idea or two from dissenters. There is little more insolent than public officials, like Mr. Bush's attorney general, who seek to silence dissent. "To those who scare peace-loving people with phantoms of lost liberty, my message is this," Attorney General Ashcroft says. "Your tactics only aid terrorists—for they erode national unity and diminish our resolve. They give ammunition to America's enemies." I commend Senator Taft's wise words to the attorney general, whose try at outlawing debate is in the deepest sense un-American.

As for the second question, the factual question, the historical record shows that our ancestors have never abstained from dissent in wartime. Even in the American Revolution, one third of the colonists, according to John Adams, opposed the drive toward independence.

At the end of the 1790s, the infant republic found itself engaged in an undeclared naval war with France. There was considerable opposition to taking arms against an ally without whom the colonists would have been hard put to win the Revolution. John Adams was by then president. He was by no means a warmonger, as many members of the Federalist Party were.

Still, he was irritated by mass protests against his policies. His wife, Abigail, called for the suppression of "wicked and base, violent and calumniating abuse . . . levelled against the government." President Adams obediently favored repression, and on July 14, 1798, he signed the Alien and Sedition Acts. The Federalists would have been better advised to call them the Patriot Acts, but in 1798 conservatives were innocent of the fine art of public relations.

The Sedition Act was expressly aimed at critics of the Adams administration, outlawing "false, scandalous and malicious" statements with intent to bring the president and the government into "contempt or disrepute, or to excite against them . . . the hatred of the good people of the United States." Alexander Hamilton to his credit opposed the Alien and Sedition Acts, but George Washington approved them.

Seventeen people were indicted under the Sedition Act, and ten were found guilty of intent to defame the president and the national government. Even a congressman, Matthew Lyon of Vermont, was convicted of writing disrespectfully about President Adams. The congressman was fined $1,000— a considerable sum in those days, probably close to $50,000 in the debased currency of the twenty-first century—and was sentenced to four months in jail. His Vermont constituents defiantly reelected him while he was still in prison, thereby serving two terms at once. In a state of panic, we often commit excesses in the name of patriotism. Then we hate ourselves in the morning. In 1840, Congress repaid Matthew Lyon's fine to his heirs. No one, not even Attorney General Ashcroft, dares defend the Alien and Sedition Acts today.

A dozen years later came the War of 1812, called by the historian Samuel Eliot Morison "the most unpopular war that this country has ever waged, not even excepting the Vietnam conflict." President Madison's request for a declaration of war against Great Britain narrowly passed the Senate by 19 to 13 votes and the House of Representatives by 70 to 49. Those votes showed trouble ahead.

After war was declared, Governor Caleb Strong of Massachusetts proclaimed a public fast to atone for a needless war "against the nation from which we are descended." Most New England governors joined Governor Strong in refusing presidential requests for state militia to reinforce the tiny federal army. "Mr. Madison's war" converted the Federalist Party, heretofore the proud champion of a strong central government, into a states' rights party with a nullificationist wing. John Quincy Adams even thought that the anti-war Hartford convention was a secessionist conspiracy aimed at a separate peace with Britain.

The Mexican War was almost as unpopular. There was fierce opposition to the declaration of war. "People of the United States!" cried the famous editor of the *New York Tribune*, Horace Greeley, "Your rulers are precipitating you into a fathomless abyss of crime and calamity! . . . Awake and arrest the work of butchery ere it shall be too late to preserve your souls from the guilt of wholesale slaughter!"

The Massachusetts legislature passed a resolution declaring that the war, "so hateful in its objects, so wanton, unjust and unconstitutional in its origin and character, must be regarded as a war against freedom, against justice, against the Union." Thoreau wrote his plea for "The Duty of Civil Disobedience," and James Russell Lowell condemned the war in his long satiric poem *Biglow Papers.* "The United States will conquer Mexico," said Ralph Waldo Emerson, "but it will be as the man swallows the arsenic, which brings him down in turn. Mexico will poison us." (Karl Marx, on the other hand, defended the war, asking sarcastically whether "it was such a misfortune that glorious California has been wrenched from the lazy Mexicans.")

In the midterm elections of 1846, the administration of James K. Polk lost thirty-five seats and control of the House of Representatives. The new House passed a resolution declaring that the Mexican War had been "unnecessarily and unconstitutionally begun by the President of the United States." Talk about giving aid and comfort to the enemy! A few days later a young congressman from the state of Illinois attacked the presidential case for the war as "from beginning to end the sheerest deception." He described President Polk as "running hither and thither, like some tortured creature, on a burning surface, finding no position, on which it can settle down." That young congressman was named Abraham Lincoln. His letter to his law partner back in Illinois, quoted in chapter 2, pointed out the constitutional and practical flaws in what we today call the Bush Doctrine.

Thirteen years later, Lincoln, now president, faced a war of his own. The Civil War saw acute divisions even in the northern states. The Copperheads—northern men with southern convictions—denounced Lincoln as a dictator and called for negotiated peace with the Confederacy. In the midterm election of 1862, the opposition gained thirty-two seats in the House, and Lincoln worried about his prospects for a second term. Ten weeks before the 1864 presidential election, he wrote: "It seems exceedingly probable that this administration will not be returned." Fortunately for the future of the republic, he won and the abolition of slavery was assured, though the opposition polled a sturdy 45 percent of the vote.

It is evident that rally-round-the-president when the nation is at war is not especially the American tradition. As history indicates, war presidents have never been exempt from criticism and dissent. The Spanish-American War and particularly the follow-up war against the independence of the newly acquired Philippines provoked biting criticism directed at William McKinley, the Republican president. In the midterm election three months after the smashing American victory over Spain, the Democrats scored impressive gains. As the McKinley administration brutally pursued the war against the Filipinos, criticism intensified.

William James, the great philosopher, explained why in the election of 1900 he supported the Democratic candidate William Jennings Bryan despite his "free silver" advocacy. "There are worse things than financial troubles in a Nation's career," James said. "To puke up its ancient soul, and the only things that gave it eminence among other nations, in five minutes and without a wink of squeamishness, is worse; and that is what the Republicans would commit us to in the Philippines. Our conduct there has been one protracted infamy towards the Islanders, and one protracted lie towards ourselves." Let us indeed wave the flag, Mark Twain said, with "the white stripes painted black, and the stars replaced by the skull and cross-bones."

The First World War was preceded by an intense national debate. Woodrow Wilson was reelected in 1916 on the ground that he kept us out of the war. The next year he called on Congress to declare war against Germany; and in the midterm election of 1918, he lost both houses of Congress to the Republican opposition.

The Wilson administration responded to criticism by enacting two laws—the Espionage Act of 1917, the Sedition Act of 1918. The Espionage Act empowered the postmaster general to ban "seditious" matters from the mails, which Wilson's postmaster general construed as anything questioning the motives of the government. The Sedition Act, as Alan Brinkley writes in *The War on Our Freedoms* (2003), the Century Foundation's valuable book on our current predicament, "made it a criminal offense to use 'any disloyal, profane, scurrilous, or abusive language about the form of government of the United States, or the Constitution of the United States, or the flag of the United States, or the uniform of the Army or Navy,' or any language that might bring those institutions 'into contempt, scorn . . . or disrepute.'" Senator

Hiram Johnson of California summed it all up: "You shall not criticize anything or anybody in the government any longer or you shall go to jail." Wilson's attorney general, the notorious A. Mitchell Palmer, protected the government against an imagined conspiracy concocted by radicals and immigrants. It was in the Palmer raids that the young J. Edgar Hoover got his start.

Once again, we hated ourselves in the morning. The reaction to Palmer's Red Scare led us to the establishment of the American Civil Liberties Union and the judicial reinforcement and expansion of the First Amendment. Though the Second World War was preceded by the angriest national debate in my lifetime—angrier than the debate over communism in the 1940s, angrier than the debate over McCarthyism in the 1950s, angrier than the debate over Vietnam in the 1960s—the civil liberties record during the Second World War was pretty good, with the glaring exception of the internment of Japanese-Americans (which, as noted, Attorney General Francis Biddle opposed).

Presidents in wartime remained objects of criticism and dissent. As we saw in chapter 1, Franklin D. Roosevelt lost seats in both houses of Congress eleven months after Pearl Harbor in the midterm election of 1942. The Korean War reduced Harry Truman, despite popular policies like the Marshall Plan, to about 25 percent approval in his last year in office. The Vietnam War drove Lyndon Johnson from the White House in 1968, despite notable achievements in domestic affairs. The year after his victory in the first Gulf War, George Bush the elder was beaten by a little known governor of Arkansas.

History thus shows there is nothing sacrosanct about war presidents. Yet there were those in the second Iraq War who promoted the idea that patriotic Americans had a moral obligation to rally round the president. This idea, as we have seen, is valid neither in principle nor in practice. Our history argues against it and demonstrates its flaws and fallacies. But in the post-9/11 atmosphere, the idea had a certain appeal. The novel and widespread conviction of personal vulnerability, the unprecedented and widespread fear of attack from the shadows, explained the impulse to seek protection in national unity behind the president.

President Bush made a drastic change in the foreign policy of the United States, a change that deserved to be debated on its merits. No national debate preceded the Iraq War of a quality and seriousness that preceded most wars in American history. This represented a failure of the political process. Once again, as after the Alien and Sedition Acts, after the Palmer raids, after the internment of Japanese- and Italian-Americans, we hated ourselves in the morning. Looking back a decade from now, I doubt that most Americans will take much pride in the fate of the 660 Guantánamo Bay "detainees" denied specification of charges, access to counsel, contact with families, and the right to a judicial hearing.

I suggested early on that our first two questions—whether a free people is obliged in wartime to shut up and obey their president; and whether our ancestors had in fact done that in the past—presuppose a third question: What is the nature of patriotism anyway?

True patriotism, I would propose, consists of living up to a nation's highest ideals. Carl Schurz, who emigrated from Germany to become a noble figure in nineteenth-century America, defined the true meaning of patriotism when he said:

"Our country, right or wrong. When right, to be kept right; when wrong, to be put right."

CHAPTER 5

HOW TO DEMOCRATIZE
AMERICAN DEMOCRACY

The true significance of the disputed 2000 election has thus far escaped public attention. This was an election that made the *loser* of the popular vote the president of the United States. But that astounding fact has been obscured: first by the flood of electoral complaints about deceptive ballots, hanging chads, and so on in Florida; then by the political astuteness of the Supreme Court–appointed president in behaving as if he had won the White House by a landslide; and later by the effect of 9/11 in presidentializing George W. Bush and giving him for a season commanding popularity in the polls.

"The fundamental maxim of republican government," observed Alexander Hamilton in *Federalist 22*, ". . . requires that the sense of the majority should prevail." A reasonable deduction from Hamilton's premise is that the presidential candidate who wins the most votes in an election should also win the election. But four times in the history of the American republic the people's choice has been denied the presidency. The ever present possibility of crowning the pop-ular-vote *loser* is surely the great anomaly in the American democratic order.

Yet the National Commission on Federal Election Reform, a body appointed in the wake of the 2000 election and co-chaired (honorarily) by former presidents Gerald Ford and Jimmy Carter, virtually ignored it. In a report opti-mistically entitled *To Assure Pride and Confidence in the Electoral Process*, the commission concluded that it had satisfactorily addressed "most of the problems that came into national view" in 2000. But nothing in the ponderous eighty-page document addressed the most fundamental problem that came into national view: the constitutional anomaly that per-mits the people's choice to be refused the presidency.

How did this anomaly arise? The answer, of course, is that the Constitution awards the presidency to the winner not of the popular vote but of the state-by-state electoral vote as registered in the electoral college. The electoral college, a last-minute addition to the Constitution, is a mystic agency hov-ering between the electorate and the presidency—impossible to explain to foreigners; even most Americans don't under-stand it.

Why the electoral college? Little consumed more time in the Constitutional Convention than debate over the mode of choosing the chief executive. The question was brought up, Professor Shlomo Slonim has calculated, on twenty-one dif-ferent days and occasioned over thirty distinct votes. James

Wilson, next only to James Madison in his influence on the proceedings, said: "The subject has greatly divided the House, and will also divide people out of doors. It is in truth the most difficult of all on which we have had to decide."

The framers, committed to the independence of the executive and to the separation of powers, rejected the proposal that Congress elect the president. Though both Madison and Wilson argued for direct election by the people, the convention, fearing the parochialism of uninformed voters, also rejected that plan. "The extent of the country," said George Mason, "renders it impossible that the people can have the requisite capacity to judge of the respective pretensions of the candidates." In an age of great distances and difficult communications, voters would tend to go for people they knew at the expense of national figures they had barely heard of.

In the end, the framers agreed on the novel device of an electoral college. Each state would appoint electors equal in number to its representation in Congress. The electors would then vote for two persons. The one receiving a majority of electoral votes would become president; the runner-up, vice president. And in a key sentence the Constitution stipulated that of these two persons, one at least should not be from the same state as the electors.

Presumably, the electors would be cosmopolitans who would know, or know of, eminences in other states. This does not mean that they were created as free agents authorized to ignore or invalidate the choice of the voters. This was not the framers' intention. Electors were expected, though not legally required, to express the will of the voters. The framers, with their talent for ambiguity, were hazy on the question of the electors' freedom to choose. Perhaps they were making tactical concessions in order to win the acquiescence of those who thought Congress should elect presidents. But the framers did not expect electors routinely to contravene the popular will. The electors, said John Clopton of Virginia, are the "organs . . . acting from a certain and unquestioned knowledge of the choice of the people, by whom they themselves were appointed, and under immediate responsibility to them."

"The president," as Madison summed it up when the convention finally adopted the electoral college, "is now to be elected by the people." The president, he assured the Virginia ratifying convention, would be "the choice of the people at large." In the First Congress, he described the president as appointed "by the suffrage of three million people." "It is desirable," Hamilton wrote in *Federalist 68*, "that the sense of the people should operate in the choice of the person to whom so important a trust was to be confided." As Lucius Wilmerding, Jr., concluded in his magisterial study of the electoral college, "The Electors were never meant to choose the president but only to pronounce the votes of the people."

The electoral system set the contours of American politics on a state-by-state basis. The electoral college's role was modified in 1804 when the Twelfth Amendment required separate votes for president and vice president. Political parties, though unknown to the Constitution and deplored by the framers, were remolding the presidential election process. By 1836, all states except South Carolina had decided to cast

their votes as a unit—winner-take-all—no matter how narrow the margin. This decision minimized the power of third
parties and created a solid foundation for a two-party system.

"The mode of appointment of the Chief Magistrate of
the United States," wrote Hamilton in the same *Federalist*, "is
almost the only part of the system, of any consequence,
which has escaped without severe censure." This may have
been true when Hamilton wrote it in 1788; it was definitely
not true thereafter. The electoral system, though reluctantly
accepted as part of the constitutional procedure, has had an
uneasy existence. According to the Congressional Research
Service, legislators since the First Congress have offered more
than a thousand proposals to alter the mode of choosing
presidents.

No one after the Constitutional Convention has advocated
the election of the president by Congress. Some have advocated modifications in the electoral college—to change the
electoral units from states to congressional districts, for example, or to require a proportional division of electoral votes.
The latter approach received some congressional favor in the
1950s in a plan proposed by Senator Henry Cabot Lodge, Jr.,
of Massachusetts and Representative Ed Gossett of Texas. The
Lodge-Gossett amendment would have ended the winner-
take-all electoral system and divided each state's electoral vote
according to the popular vote. In 1950, the Senate endorsed
the amendment by more than the two thirds required by the
Constitution, but the House turned it down. Five years later,
Senator Estes Kefauver of Tennessee revived the Lodge-
Gossett plan and won the backing of the Senate Judiciary

Committee. A thoughtful debate ensued, with Senators John F. Kennedy of Massachusetts and Paul H. Douglas of Illinois leading the opposition and defeating the amendment.

Each state, however, retains the constitutional right to appoint its electors "in such manner as the legislature thereof directs." In 2000, two states, Maine and Nebraska, split their electoral votes—two going to the winner of the statewide vote; the rest to the popular-vote winner in each congressional district. The other states kept the unit rule.

But neither the district plan nor the proportionate plan would prevent a popular-vote loser from winning the White House. To correct this great anomaly of the Constitution, many have advocated the abolition of the electoral college and its replacement by direct popular elections.

The first minority president was John Quincy Adams. In the 1824 election, Andrew Jackson led in both popular and electoral votes but, with four candidates dividing the electoral vote, failed to win an electoral college majority. The Constitution provides that, if no candidate has a majority, the House of Representatives must choose among the top three. Speaker of the House Henry Clay, who came in fourth, threw his support to Adams, thereby making him president. When Adams then made Clay his secretary of state, Jacksonian cries of "corrupt bargain" filled the air for the next four years and helped Jackson win the electoral college majority in 1828.

Jackson was the first president to confront the constitutional anomaly and to call for direct popular elections. "The first principle of our system," Jackson told Congress in 1829, is that "*the majority is to govern*. . . . To the people belongs the right of electing their Chief Magistrate." "Experience proves," he continued—the experience in his own mind no doubt that of his 1824 defeat in the House of Representatives—"that in proportion as agents to execute the will of the people are multiplied there is danger of their wishes being frustrated." He asked for the removal of all "intermediate" agencies preventing "the expression for the will of the majority. . . . It is safer for them to express their own will." The winner of the popular vote had the overriding claim to democratic legitimacy.

Jackson added in tacit verdict on Adams's failed administration, "A President elected by a minority can not enjoy the confidence necessary to the successful discharge of his duties." History bears out Jackson's point. The next two minority presidents—Rutherford B. Hayes in 1877, Benjamin Harrison in 1889—had, like Adams, ineffectual administrations. All suffered setbacks in their midterm congressional elections. None won a second term in the White House.

The most recent president to propose a direct-election amendment was Jimmy Carter in 1977. The amendment, he said, would "ensure that the candidate chosen by the voters actually becomes president. Under the electoral college, it is always possible that the winner of the popular vote will not be elected." This had already happened, Carter said, in 1824, 1876, and 1888.

Actually, Carter placed too much historical blame on the electoral college. Neither J. Q. Adams in 1824 nor Rutherford B. Hayes in 1876 owed his elevation to the electoral college. The House of Representatives, as we have seen, elected Adams. Hayes's victory was more complicated.

In 1876, Samuel J. Tilden, the Democratic candidate, won the popular vote, and it appeared that he had won the electoral vote too. But the Confederate states were still under military occupation, and electoral boards in Florida, Louisiana, and South Carolina disqualified Democratic ballots in order to give Hayes the electoral majority.

The Republicans controlled the Senate, the Democrats the House. Which body would count the electoral votes? To resolve the deadlock, Congress appointed an electoral commission. By an 8–7 party-line vote, the commission gave all the disputed votes to Hayes. Three days before the inauguration, the electoral college by a single vote declared Hayes the next president. But it was the rigged electoral commission, not the electoral college, that denied the popular-vote winner the presidency. This was a supreme election swindle, and there was a season of great bitterness. But the compromise of 1877 appeased Democrats by terminating Reconstruction and turning the South over to the ex-Confederates.

In 1888, the electoral college did deprive the popular-vote winner, Grover Cleveland, of victory. But 1888 was a clouded election. Neither candidate received a majority, and Cleveland's margin was only 95,000 votes. The claim was made, and was widely accepted at the time and by scholars since, that white election officials in the South banned perhaps 300,000 black Republicans from the polls. In the North, as the chairman of the Republican National Committee observed, Harrison would "never know how close a number of men were compelled to approach the gates of the penitentiary to make him president." Fraud tainted the results both North and South. The installation of a minority president in 1889 took place without serious protest.

The republic went through several further elections in which a small shift of votes would have given the popular-vote loser an electoral college victory. In 1916, if Charles Evans Hughes had gained 4,000 votes more in California, he would have won the electoral college majority, though he lost the popular vote to Woodrow Wilson by more than half a million. In 1948, a shift of fewer than 30,000 votes in three states would have given Thomas E. Dewey the electoral college majority, though he ran more than 2 million votes behind Harry Truman. In 1976, a shift of 8,000 votes in two states would have made Gerald Ford president, though he ran more than 1.5 million votes behind Jimmy Carter.

Many eminent politicos and organizations have joined Jackson and Carter in advocating direct popular elections—Presidents Richard Nixon and Gerald Ford, Vice Presidents Alben Barkley and Hubert Humphrey, Senators Robert A. Taft, Mike Mansfield, Edward Kennedy, Henry Jackson, Robert Dole, Howard Baker, Everett Dirksen; the American Bar Association, the League of Women Voters, the AFL-CIO, the United States Chamber of Commerce. Polls showed overwhelming public support for direct elections. The Gallup Poll in June 1944 recorded 65 percent in favor, 23 percent opposed (the rest had no opinion); in 1967, it was 58 to 22 percent.

In the late 1960s, the direct-election amendment achieved

a certain momentum. The campaign was led by Senator Birch Bayh of Indiana, an inveterate and persuasive constitutional reformer, and it was fueled by the fear that Governor George Wallace of Alabama might win enough electoral votes in 1968 to throw the election into the House of Representatives. In May 1968 Gallup recorded 66 percent in favor of direct elections and in November an astonishing 80 percent.

In 1969, the House of Representatives approved a direct-election amendment by the impressive vote of 338 to 70. But the next year a filibuster killed the amendment in the Senate. Wallace's 46 electoral votes in 1968 had not been enough to deny Richard Nixon a majority, and an unjustified complacency soon took over. "The decline in one-party states," a Brookings Institution study concluded in 1970, "has made it far less likely today that the runner-up in popular votes will be elected president."

Polls continued to show popular support for direct elections—73 percent in 1977, 67 percent in 1980. But because the danger of electoral college misfire seemed academic, abolition of the college became once again a low-priority issue: "Nobody has a kind word for the outmoded electoral college," wrote the journalist Robert Bendiner, "but only professors and cartoonists get really worked up about it."

Then came the election of 2000. Here was a flagrant example of the structural anomaly in the American polity. For the fourth time in American history, the winner of the popular vote was denied the presidency. And Albert Gore, Jr., had won the popular vote—not by Grover Cleveland's dubious 95,000—but by more than half a million. Another 2.8

million votes had gone to the third-party candidate, Ralph Nader, making the alleged victor, George W. Bush, more than ever a minority president.

Nor was Bush's victory in the electoral college unclouded by doubt. The electoral vote turned on a single state: Florida. Five members of the Supreme Court, forsaking their usual deference to state sovereignty, stopped the Florida recount and thereby made Bush president. Critics derided the Court's decision. They wondered whether, if the facts had been the same but the candidates reversed, with Bush winning the popular vote (as indeed observers had rather expected) and Gore hoping to win the electoral vote, the gang of five would have found the same legal arguments to elect Gore that they used to elect Bush.

I expected an explosion of public outrage over the rejection of the people's choice. But there was surprisingly little in the way of outcry. In July 2001 the Oregon Democratic central committee, spurred on by former Congressman Charles O. Porter, passed a resolution petitioning Congress to determine whether the gang of five on the Supreme Court should be impeached for their partisan intervention in the election. The proposal got nowhere.

For one thing, the new president, avoiding J. Q. Adams's acknowledgment of a deficit in public confidence, acted as if he had won a mandate. This was politically astute, and voters, weary after the prolonged electoral agony and eager to get on with their lives, accepted Bush's claim to legitimacy.

Another factor was the tepid reaction to the Gore candidacy. It is hard to imagine such popular acquiescence in a popular-vote loser presidency if the popular-vote winner had been, say, Adlai Stevenson or John F. Kennedy or Ronald Reagan. Such leaders attracted do-or-die supporters, voters who cared intensely about them and who would not only have questioned the result but would have been ardent in defense of their favorites. After a disappointing campaign, Vice President Gore simply did not excite the same impassioned commitment.

Justice Stephen Breyer, part of the Court's dissenting minority, suggested another factor in remarks before the American Bar Association in August 2001. The absence of outrage, Breyer was reported as saying, was evidence of the faith of Americans in their system of justice. The acceptance of the Court's 5–4 presidential choice, Breyer said, demonstrated "that losers as well as winners will abide by the result, and so will the public."

Of course there was no alternative to abiding by the result. But the absence of outrage made the search for reform technical rather than constitutional. Diverse commissions, official and unofficial, focused their reform interests on such topics as voting machines, ballot design, voter registration, access to the polls, absentee ballots, media reporting of election results, and uniform national standards for these and other matters. They did not focus at all on the most vital question posed by the 2000 election: the role of the electoral system as a subversion of democracy.

The modernization of electoral technology will no doubt produce a more accurate and efficient expression of voters' preferences. But it will not touch the great anomaly of the

Constitution. Nothing in the technical reforms will prevent the rejection of the people's choice once again in the future.

Yet surely the 2000 election put the republic in an intolerable predicament—intolerable because the result contravened the theory of democracy. Many expected that the election would resurrect the movement for a constitutional amendment mandating direct election of presidents. Since direct elections have obvious democratic plausibility and since few Americans understand the electoral college anyway, its abolition seems a logical remedy.

The resurrection has not taken place. Constitutional reformers are intimidated by the argument that the direct-election amendment will antagonize the small states and therefore cannot be ratified. It would necessarily eliminate the special advantage conferred on small states by the two electoral votes handed to all states whatever their population. Small-state opposition, it is claimed, would make it impossible to collect the two thirds of Congress and the three fourths of the states required for ratification.

This is an odd argument because political analysts argue that the electoral college in fact benefits large states, not small states. Far from being hurt by direct elections, small states, they say, would benefit from them. "The idea that the present electoral college preserves the power of the small states," write Lawrence D. Longley and Alan G. Braun in *The Politics of Electoral College Reform* (1975), ". . . simply is not the case." The electoral college system "benefits large states, urban interests, white minorities, and/or black voters." So too the Brookings report of 1970: "Advocates of the existing system approve of the power it gives to populous states. . . . The decline of the metropolitan bloc would be the most important change [brought about by direct elections]. For several decades, liberal, urban Democrats and progressive, urban-suburban Republicans have tended to dominate presidential politics; they would lose influence under the direct-vote plan."

Minorities holding the balance of power in large states agree that the abolition of the electoral college would be disadvantageous. "Take away the electoral college," said Vernon Jordan as president of the Urban League, "and the importance of being black melts away. Blacks, instead of being crucial to victory in major states, simply become 10 percent of the electorate, with reduced impact."

And it is an odd argument too because the small vs. large state lineup has practically vanished since the Constitutional Convention. "None of the great battles of American political history—in Congress or in Presidential elections," the journalist Neal Pierce has pointed out, "has been fought on a basis of small versus large states."

The debate over whom direct elections would benefit—large states? small states? urban interests? rural interests? whites? blacks? latinos?—has been long, wearisome, contradictory, and inconclusive. Even computer calculations assume a static political culture. They do not take into account, nor can they predict, the changes wrought in voter dynamics by candidates, issues, and events.

As Senator John Kennedy said during the Lodge-Gossett debate, "It is not only the unit vote for the presidency we are talking about, but a whole solar system of governmental power. If it is proposed to change the balance of power of one of the elements of the solar system, it is necessary to consider all the others. . . . What the effects of these various changes will be on the federal system, the two-party system, the popular plurality system and the large-state-small-state checks and balances system, no one knows."

Direct elections have at least the merit of correcting the great anomaly of the Constitution and providing an escape from the intolerable predicament. The arguments for the direct-election plan are indeed powerful. "The electoral college method of electing a president of the United States," said the American Bar Association, "is archaic, complex, ambiguous, indirect, and dangerous." "Direct popular election of the president," said Birch Bayh, "is the only system that is truly democratic, truly equitable, and can truly reflect the will of the people."

The plan meets the moral criteria of a democracy. It would elect the people's choice. It would ensure equal treatment of all votes. It would reduce the power of sectionalism in politics. It would reinvigorate party competition and combat voter apathy by giving parties the incentive to get out their votes in states that they have no hope of carrying.

The abolition of the electoral college would also solve the problem of the "faithless elector"—the person who is sent to the electoral college to vote for one candidate and then votes for another. This has happened from time to time in the past, could happen again, and might even change the outcome when the electoral vote is closely divided.

The direct-election plan sounds reasonable. Its objectives

are excellent. But direct elections raise troubling problems of their own, especially their impact on the party system and on JFK's "solar system of governmental power."

In the nineteenth century, visiting Europeans were awed by the American commitment to politics. Alexis de Tocqueville in the 1830s thought politics "the only pleasure an American knows." James Bryce half a century later was impressed by the "military discipline" of American parties. Voting statistics justified transatlantic awe. In no presidential election between the Civil War and the end of the century did turnout fall below 70 percent of eligible voters.

The dutiful citizens of these high-turnout years did not rush to the polls out of uncontrollable excitement over the choices they were about to make. The dreary procession of presidential candidates moved Bryce to write his famous chapter in *The American Commonwealth* on "Why Great Men Are Not Chosen President." But the party was supremely effective as an agency of voter mobilization. Party loyalty was intense. People were as likely to switch parties as they were to switch churches. The great difference between then and now is the decay of the party as the organizing unit of American politics.

The modern history of parties has been the steady loss of the functions that gave parties their classical role. Civil service reform largely dried up the reservoir of patronage. Social legislation reduced the need for parties to succor the poor and helpless. Mass entertainment gave people more agreeable diversions than listening to political harangues. Party loyalty became tenuous; party identification casual. As Franklin D.

Roosevelt observed in 1940, "The growing independence of voters, after all, has been proven by the votes in every presidential election since my childhood—and the tendency, frankly, is on the increase."

Since FDR's day, a fundamental transformation in the political environment has further undermined the shaky structure of American politics. Two electronic devices—television and computerized polling—have had a devastating impact on the party system. The old system had three tiers: the politician at one end; the voter at the other; the party in between. The party's function was to negotiate between the politician and the voter, interpreting each to the other and providing the links that held the political process together.

The electronic revolution has substantially abolished this mediatorial role. Television presents politicians directly to voters, who judge candidates far more on what the box shows them than on what the party organization tells them. Computerized polls present voters directly to politicians, who judge the electorate far more on what the polls show them than on what the party organization tells them. The political party is left to wither on the vine.

The last half century has been notable for the decrease in party identification, for the increase in independent voting, and for the number of independent presidential candidacies by fugitives from the major parties: Henry Wallace and Strom Thurmond in 1948, George Wallace in 1968, Eugene McCarthy in 1976, John Anderson in 1980, Ross Perot in 1992 and 1996, Ralph Nader and Pat Buchanan in 2000, Nader in 2004.

The two-party system has been a source of stability. FDR called it "one of the greatest methods of unification and of teaching people to think in common terms." The alternative to the party system would be a slow, agonized descent into an era of what the political scientist Walter Dean Burnham has termed "politics without parties." Political adventurers might roam the countryside like Afghan warlords, building personal armies equipped with electronic technologies, conducting hostilities against some rival warlords, forming alliances with others, and, if they win elections, striving to govern through ad hoc coalitions. Accountability would fade away. Without the stabilizing influence of parties, American politics would grow angrier, wilder, and more irresponsible.

The abolition of state-by-state, winner-take-all electoral votes would hasten the disintegration of the party system. Minor parties have a dim future in the electoral college. Unless third parties have a solid regional base, like the Populists of 1892 or the Dixiecrats of 1948, they cannot hope to win electoral votes. Millard Fillmore, the Know-Nothing candidate of 1856, won 21.6 percent of the popular vote and only 2 percent of the electoral vote. In 1912, when Theodore Roosevelt's candidacy turned the Republicans into a third party, William Howard Taft carried 23 percent of the popular vote and only 1.5 percent of the electoral vote.

But the direct-election plan, by enabling minor parties to accumulate votes from state to state—impossible in the electoral college system—would give them a new role and new power. Direct-election advocates recognize that encouragement of splinter candidates and parties would drain votes away from the major parties. Most direct-election amendments, therefore, provide that, if no candidate receives 40 percent of the vote, the two top candidates would fight it out in a runoff election.

Direct elections would offer potent incentives to radical zealots (e.g., Ralph Nader), freelance media adventurers (e.g., Pat Buchanan), eccentric billionaires (e.g., Ross Perot), flamboyant characters (e.g., Jesse Ventura) to jump into presidential contests; incentives too to green parties, pro-choice parties, anti-gun-control parties, homosexual rights parties, prohibition parties, and so on down the single issue line.

Splinter parties would multiply not because they expected to win elections but because their accumulated votes would increase their bargaining power in the inevitable runoff. Their multiplication would very likely make runoffs the rule rather than the exception. One national election is alarming enough; a double national election is a fate almost too grim to contemplate.

Splinter parties would aim to extract concessions from the runoff candidates in exchange for pledges of support. Think of the skulduggery that would take place between the first and second rounds of a presidential election! Like J. Q. Adams in 1824, the victor would become a new target for "corrupt bargains."

Direct elections would very probably bring to the White House candidates who did not get anywhere near a majority of the popular vote. The prospect would be a succession of 41 percent presidents or else a succession of double national elections. Moreover, the winner in the first round might often be beaten in the second round, depending on the deals the runoff candidates made with the splinter parties. This result would hardly strengthen the sense of legitimacy the presidential election is supposed to provide. Nor have I mentioned the problem in close elections of organizing a nation-wide recount.

In short, direct elections promise a murky political future. They would further weaken the party system and further destabilize American politics. They would cure the intolerable predicament, but the cure might be worse than the disease.

Are we therefore stuck with the great anomaly of the Constitution? Is no remedy possible?

There is a simple and effective way to avoid the troubles promised by the direct-election plan and at the same time to attain its objectives—that is, to prevent the popular-vote loser from being the electoral-vote winner. The solution is to award the popular-vote winner a bonus of two electoral votes for each state and the District of Columbia. This is the national bonus plan proposed in 1978 by the Twentieth Century Fund Task Force on Reform of the Presidential Election Process.

Under the bonus plan, a national pool of 102 new electoral votes would be awarded to the winner of the popular vote. This national bonus would balance the existing state bonus—the two electoral votes already conferred by the Constitution on each state regardless of population. The reform would virtually guarantee that the popular-vote winner would also be the electoral-vote winner.

At the same time, by retaining state electoral votes and the unit rule, the plan would preserve both the constitutional and practical role of the states in presidential elections. By insulating recounts, it would simplify the consequences of close elections. By discouraging multiplication of parties and candidates, the plan would protect the party system. By encouraging parties to maximize their vote in states they have no chance of winning, it would reinvigorate state parties, stimulate turnout, and enhance voter equality. The national bonus plan, combining the advantages of the historic system with the assurance that the winner of the popular vote would win the election, would contribute to the vitality of federalism.

The problem of the "faithless elector" can be easily solved by abolishing individual electors while retaining the electoral vote and the unit rule. There is the further problem, affirmed by the Supreme Court in *Bush v. Gore*, that the individual citizen "has no federal constitutional right to vote for electors for president unless and until the state legislature chooses statewide election." Individuals in 135 nations enjoy the constitutional right to vote, but, Professor Jamin B. Raskin tells us, the United States joins Iran, Iraq, Libya, Pakistan, Chechnya, and a few other backward countries in neglecting to recognize that fundamental right in their constitutions. This should have been corrected long since.

The national bonus plan would be a basic but a contained reform. It would fit comfortably into the historic structure. It would not derange or unbalance JFK's "solar system of governmental power." It would vindicate "the fundamental maxim of republican government . . . that the sense of the majority should prevail." It would make the American democracy live up to its democratic pretensions.

How many popular-vote losers will we have to send to the White House before we finally democratize American democracy?

CHAPTER 6

HAS DEMOCRACY
A FUTURE?

The twentieth century was no doubt, as Isaiah Berlin said, "the most terrible century in Western history." Two world wars carried death and destruction to the far corners of the planet with 160 million people killed in violent conflict and millions more killed by the monstrous whims of dictators. Churchill spoke of "the woe and ruin of the terrible twentieth century." The chronicles of human wreckage—the Holocaust and the Gulag Archipelago—haunt us still.

But this terrible century had, or seemed to have, a happy ending. As in melodramas of old, the maiden democracy, bound by villains to the railroad track, is rescued in the nick of time from the onrushing train. As the century drew to a close, both major villains had perished—fascism with a bang, communism with a whimper.

A season of triumphalism followed. Two centuries ago,

Immanuel Kant argued in his *Idea for a Universal History* that the republican form of government was destined to supersede all others. At last the prophecy seemed on the way to fulfillment. Savants hailed "the end of history." "For the first time in all history," President Clinton declared in his second inaugural address, "more people on this planet live under democracy than dictatorship." The *New York Times*, after careful checking, approved: 3.1 billion people live in democracies, 2.66 billion do not. According to end-of-history doctrine as expounded by its prophet, Francis Fukayama, the world could look forward to "the universalization of Western liberal democracy as the final form of human government."

For historians, this euphoria rang a bell of memory. Did not the same radiant hope accompany the transition from the nineteenth to the twentieth century? This most terrible hundred years in Western history started out in an atmosphere of optimism and high expectation. People of goodwill in 1900 believed in the inevitability of democracy, the invincibility of progress, the decency of human nature, and the coming reign of reason and peace. David Starr Jordan, the president of Stanford University, expressed the mood in his turn-of-the-century book *The Call of the Twentieth Century*. "The man of the Twentieth Century," Jordan predicted, "will be a hopeful man. He will love the world and the world will love him."

Looking back, we recall a century marked a good deal less by love than by hate, irrationality, and atrocity, one that for a long dark passage inspired the gravest forebodings about the very survival of the human race. Democracy, striding confidently into the 1900s, found itself almost at once on the defensive. In the second decade, the Great War, exposing the pretension that democracy would guarantee peace, shattered old structures of security and order and unleashed angry energies of revolution—revolution not for democracy but against it. Bolshevism in Russia, Fascism in Italy, Nazism in Germany, militarism in Japan, all despised, denounced, and, wherever they could, destroyed individual rights and the processes of self-government.

In the fourth decade, the Great Depression came along to expose the pretension that democracy would guarantee prosperity. A third of the way into the century, democracy seemed a helpless thing, spiritless, paralyzed, doomed. Contempt for democracy spread among elites and masses alike: contempt for parliamentary dithering, for "talking-shops," for liberties of expression and opposition, for bourgeois civility and cowardice, for pragmatic muddling through.

In the fifth decade, the Second World War threatened to administer the coup de grâce. Liberal society, its back to the wall, fought for its life. There was considerable defeatism in the West. The title of Anne Morrow Lindbergh's 1940 bestseller proclaimed totalitarianism *The Wave of the Future*. It was, she wrote, a "new, and perhaps even ultimately good, conception of humanity trying to come to birth." Hitlerism and Stalinism were merely "scum on the wave of the future. . . . The wave of the future is coming and there is no fighting it." By 1941 only about a dozen democracies were left on the planet.

The political, economic, and moral failures of democracy had handed the initiative to totalitarianism. Something like this could happen again. If liberal democracy fails in the twenty-first century, as it failed in the twentieth, to construct a humane, prosperous, and peaceful world, it will invite the rise of alternative creeds apt to be based, like fascism and communism, on flight from freedom and surrender to authority.

After all, democracy in its modern version—representative government, party competition, the secret ballot, all founded on guarantees of individual rights and freedoms—is at most two hundred years old. A majority of the world's inhabitants may be living under democracy, but democratic hegemony is a mere flash in the long, sad annals of recorded history. James Bryce, the author of *The American Commonwealth*, was an acute student of modern democracies. "We are not yet entitled," Bryce wisely said of democracy, "to hold with the men of 1789 that it is the natural and therefore in the long run the inevitable form of government. . . . A study of the various forms government has taken cannot but raise the question what ground there is for the assumption that democracy is in its final form, an unwarranted assumption, for whatever else history teaches, it gives no ground for expecting finality in any human institution."

I wonder how effectively, in the years since the collapse of the totalitarian challenges, democracy has sunk roots in previously nondemocratic countries. Fareed Zakaria has called attention to the phenomenon of "illiberal democracy"—free elections bringing to power leaders who then suppress free speech, the free press, and freedom of political opposition. Democracy, Zakaria argues, does not necessarily bring about constitutional liberalism, especially in the Third World. Even in the developed world, where democracy may have a solid traditional and constitutional base, liberal regimes still confront pent-up energies that threaten to blow them off course; even perhaps to drive them onto the rocks.

Modern democracy itself is the political offspring of technology and capitalism, the two most dynamic—that is to say, destabilizing—forces loose in the world today. Both are driven ever onward by self-generated momentum that strains the bonds of social control and of political sovereignty.

Technology created the clock, the printing press, the compass, the steam engine, the power loom, and the other innovations that laid the foundation for capitalism and that in time generated rationalism, individualism, and democracy. At first technological advance was unsystematic and intermittent. Soon it was institutionalized. "The greatest invention of the nineteenth century," said Alfred North Whitehead, "was the invention of the method of invention."

In the twentieth century, scientific and technological innovation increased at an exponential rate. Henry Adams, the most brilliant of American historians, meditated on the acceleration of history. "The world did not double or treble its movement between 1800 and 1900," Adams wrote in 1909, "but, measured by any standard . . . the tension and vibration and volume and so-called progression of society were fully a thousand times greater in 1900 than in 1800—the force had doubled ten times over, and the speed, when measured by electrical standards as in telegraphy, approached infinity, and had annihilated both space and time." Nothing, Adams thought, could slow this process, for "the law of acceleration . . . cannot be supposed to relax its energy to suit the convenience of man."

The law of acceleration hurtles us into a new historical epoch. The present shift from a factory-based economy to a computer-based economy is even more profound than the shift technology forced on our great-great-grandparents two centuries ago from a farm-based to a factory-based economy. The Industrial Revolution extended over generations and allowed time for human and institutional adjustment. The Computer Revolution is far swifter, far more compressed, far more dynamic in tempo, far more traumatic in impact.

The computer will affect the procedures of democratic politics. James Madison in *The Federalist Papers* distinguished between "pure democracy," by which he meant a system in which citizens assemble and administer the government in person, and a republic, by which he meant a system in which the majority expresses its will through "a scheme of representation." For most of American history, "pure democracy" was necessarily limited to town meetings in small villages. Now the interactivity introduced by the Computer Revolution makes "pure democracy" technically feasible on a national scale. The rise of public opinion polls, focus groups, and referendums suggests popular demand for direct democracy. With a nation of computers plugged into the Internet, "pure democracy" seems just around the corner. Plebiscitary democracy, direct democracy, cyberdemocracy, the electronic town hall: under whatever name, is this a desirable prospect?

Perhaps not. Interactivity encourages instant responses, discourages second thoughts, and offers outlets for demagoguery, egomania, insult, and hate. Listen to talk radio! In too interactive a polity, a "common passion," as Madison feared, could sweep through a people and lead to emotional and ill-judged actions. Remember the explosion of popular indignation when President Truman fired General Douglas MacArthur: 78,000 letters descended on the White House running 20–1 against the president. But representative institutions compelled second thoughts, and the principle of civilian control of the military was soon vindicated. One is grateful that the electronic town hall was not running the country in 1951. The Internet has done little thus far to foster the reasoned exchanges that in Madison's words "refine and enlarge the public views."

While the onrush of technology creates new substantive problems and promises to revise the political system through which we deal with them, the onrush of capitalism may have even more disruptive consequences. Let us understand the relationship between capitalism and democracy. Democracy is impossible without private ownership because private property—resources beyond the arbitrary reach of the state—provides the only secure basis for political opposition and intellectual freedom. But the capitalist market is no guarantee of democracy, as Deng Xiaoping, Lee Kuan Yew, Pinochet, and Franco, not to mention Hitler and Mussolini, have amply demonstrated. Democracy requires capitalism, but capitalism does not require democracy.

Capitalism has proved itself the supreme engine of innovation, production, and distribution. But its method, as it careens ahead, heedless of little beyond its own profits, is what

Joseph Schumpeter called "creative destruction." In its economic theory, capitalism rests on the concept of equilibrium. In practice, its very dynamism, its very irrational exuberance, drive it forever toward disequilibrium. "Stationary capitalism," as Schumpeter said, "is a contradiction in terms." This is the dilemma of contemporary conservatism. The unfettered market conservatives worship undermines the values—stability, morality, family, community, work, discipline, delayed gratification—conservatives avow. The glitter of the fast buck, the greed, the short-termism, the exploitation of prurient appetites, the ease of fraud, the devil-take-the-hindmost ethos—all are at war with purported conservative ideals.

Even premier capitalists are appalled by what runaway capitalism has wrought. If understanding of capitalism can be measured by success in making money out of it, no one understands contemporary capitalism better than the financier and philanthropist George Soros. "Although I have made a fortune in the financial markets," Soros writes, "I now fear that the untrammeled intensification of laissez-faire capitalism and the spread of market values into all areas of life is endangering our open and democratic society." The "uninhibited pursuit of self-interest," Soros continues, results in "intolerable inequities and instability." The villain is "market fundamentalism."

The Computer Revolution offers wondrous new possibilities for creative destruction. One goal of capitalist creativity is the globalized economy. One—unplanned—candidate for capitalist destruction is the nation-state, the traditional site of democracy. The computer turns the untrammeled market into a global juggernaut crashing across frontiers, enfeebling national powers of taxation and regulation, undercutting national management of interest rates and exchange rates, widening disparities of wealth both within and between nations, dragging down labor standards, degrading the environment, denying nations the shaping of their own economic destiny, accountable to no one, creating a world economy without a world polity. Cyberspace is beyond national control. No authorities exist to provide international control. Where is democracy now?

There are other pent-up energies. The most fateful source in the United States is race. "The problem of the twentieth century," W. E. B. Du Bois observed in 1900, "is the problem of the color line." His prediction will come to full flower in the twenty-first century. Minorities seek full membership in the larger American society. Doors slammed in their faces, crosses burned on their lawns, drive them to protest, sometimes to violence. The revolt against white racism took time to gather strength. White America, belatedly awakening to cruelties so long practiced against people of color, tries now to compensate by enacting significant reforms—but then is irritated to find that reform often leads to the intensification of protest. As Tocqueville explained long ago, "Patiently endured so long as it seemed beyond redress, a grievance comes to appear intolerable once the possibility of removing it crosses men's minds. For the mere fact that certain abuses have been remedied draws attention to others, and they now appear more galling; people may suffer less, but their sensibility is exacerbated."

The end of the Eurocentric era raises further problems for democracy. Self-government, individual rights, equality before the law are European inventions. Now the age of the Pacific is upon us. The breakthrough of Japan in the century just ended heralds the breakthrough of China and India in the century ahead. Present economic troubles will pass, and the magnetism of Asia will alter the contours of the global economy, foreshadowing historic shifts in the planetary balance of power.

The Asian tradition, we are told, values the group more than the individual, order more than debate, authority more than liberty, solidarity more than freedom. Some Asian leaders, notably Lee Kuan Yew of Singapore and Mahathir bin Mohamad of Malaysia, love to contrast Asian discipline and stability with the disorder and decadence they impute to the individualistic West. They denounce the attempt to hold Asian countries to Western democratic standards as the new form of Western imperialism.

Nevertheless, both India and Japan are functioning democracies. If the claim that human rights are universal is proof of Western arrogance, the restriction of those rights to Europe and the Americas brands non-Western peoples as lesser breeds incapable of appreciating personal liberty and self-government, and that is surely Western arrogance too. In fact, many Asians fight for human rights, and at the risk of their freedom and their lives. "Why do we assume," asks Christopher Patten, the last British governor of Hong Kong, "that Lee Kuan Yew is the embodiment of Asian values rather than Daw Aung San Suu Kyi," the courageous opposition leader under prolonged house arrest in Burma? A pre–Tiananmen Square wall poster in Beijing proclaimed: "We cannot tolerate that human rights and democracy are only slogans of the Western bourgeoisie and the Eastern proletariat only needs dictatorship." In the words of the Indian economist Amartya Sen, "The so-called Asian values that are invoked to justify authoritarianism are not especially Asian in any significant sense." Chris Patten concludes, "I think the Asian value debate is piffle. What are these Asian values? When you home in on what one or two Asian leaders mean by them, what they actually mean is that anyone who disagrees with me should shut up."

Still, the new salience of Asia on the world scene, the absence of historical predilections for democracy, and the self-interest of rulers who see democracy as a threat to their power suggest a period of Asian resistance to the spread of the democratic idea.

That resistance will be reinforced by the defensive reaction around the planet to relentless globalization—a reaction that takes the form of rejection of modernity. The world today is torn in opposite directions. Globalization is in the saddle and rides mankind, but at the same time drives people to seek refuge from its powerful force beyond their control and comprehension. They retreat into familiar, intelligible, protective units. They crave the politics of identity. The faster the world integrates, the more people will huddle in fundamentalist religious or ethnic or tribal enclaves. Integration and disintegration feed on each other.

The twentieth century was the century of secular fanaticism—communism and fascism. Secular fanatics worshipped history as their means of salvation. Secular fanaticism is therefore susceptible to disproof when history itself refutes its creeds. The twenty-first century promises, however, to be the century of religious fanaticism. Religious fanatics worship the supernatural, and religious fanaticism is therefore not susceptible to disproof because true believers never return from heaven (or hell) to testify.

Religious fanaticism is the breeding place for the greatest current threat to civilization, which is terrorism. Most of the killing around the world—whether in Ireland, Kosovo, Israel, Palestine, Kashmir, Sri Lanka, Indonesia, the Philippines, Tibet—is the consequence of religious disagreement. There are no more dangerous people on earth than those who believe they are executing the will of the Almighty. It is this conviction that drives on terrorists to murder the infidel. When suicide bombers die, they believe they are sure to catch the next train to Paradise. In vain did Lincoln observe, "The Almighty has his own purposes."

Nor is the fundamentalist revival confined to the Third World. Many people living lives of quiet desperation in modern societies hunger for transcendent meaning and turn to inerrant faith for solace and support. According to a 1995 Gallup Poll, more than a third of American adults claim that God speaks to them personally. One hopes it is the God of love rather than the God of wrath on the other end of the line. Fanaticism is the mortal enemy of that genial mix of civility, comity, and compromise that keeps democracy on the track.

Back to the question: Has democracy a future? Sure it

does, but not the glorious, irresistible, inevitable future predicted in the triumphalist moment. Democracy has survived the twentieth century by the skin of its teeth. It will not enjoy a free ride through the century to come.

Our own country, the last remaining superpower, is presumably in the best position to run the gauntlet of challenges. Yet we have troubles too. The most crucial problem for us is still Du Bois's color line. I would hazard the guess that the national capacity to absorb and assimilate newcomers is still powerful and each year embraces more oldcomers of other colors. The call of the mainstream appeals far more, above all to the young, than imprisonment in linguistic or racial ghettos. As Gunnar Myrdal put it in his great work on the race question, *An American Dilemma*: "The minority peoples of the United States are fighting for status in the larger society; the minorities of Europe are mainly fighting for independence from it." Our problem is not rejection of the white majority by minorities but rejection of minorities by the white majority.

Tensions continue, but they are increasingly mitigated by the wonderfully rising rate of intermarriage between people of different ancestries, creeds, and colors. More Japanese-Americans marry Caucasians than they do other Japanese-Americans. So many Jewish Americans marry non-Jews that the future of the Jewish community is in doubt. Over 40 percent of Hispanic-Americans between the ages of twenty-six and thirty-four marry non-Hispanics. Marriages between whites and blacks have tripled in the last thirty years. We may therefore, I think, count on sex—and love —to arrest the disuniting of America.

Despite predictions to the contrary, English will continue as the primary and dominant language. Indeed, in essentials the national character will be recognizably much as it has been in the past. People seeking clues to the American mystery will still read, and quote, Tocqueville.

Technology will rush on according to Henry Adams's law of acceleration, throwing off both dazzling new possibilities and disquieting new problems. But for all the popularity of interactive computer networks and all the unpopularity of elected officials, I doubt that Americans will permit the degradation of representative democracy into a parade of plebiscites.

Capitalism too will career on, through downs as well as ups, but laissez-faire ideology in its extreme form will probably wane as capitalists discover the range of troubles the unfettered market cannot solve, or makes worse. Market fundamentalism, with growing economic disparities at home and jobs exported abroad, excites social resentment and revives class warfare. To save the system, capitalists must begin to coordinate short-term plans and profits with such long-term social necessities as investment in education, research and development, environmental protection, health care, infrastructure, and the redemption of the inner city. Capitalists are not likely to do this on their own. Longer-term perspectives demand public leadership and a measure of affirmative government.

In the world at large, can capitalism, once loose from national moorings, be held to social accountability? Will international institutions acquire the authority to impose, for example, a global Securities and Exchange Commission? This won't happen next week, but continuing abuse of power will build a constituency for reform.

Nation-states will continue to decline as effective power units: too small for the big problem, as Daniel Bell has said, and too big for the small problems. Despite this decline, nationalism will persist as the most potent of political emotions. Whether democracy, a Western creation, can be transplanted to parts of the world with different cultures and traditions is far from certain. Yet I would expect a gradual expansion of democratic institutions and ideals. It is hard to believe that the instinct for political and intellectual freedom is limited to a happy few around the North Atlantic littoral.

Democracy in the twenty-first century must manage the pressures of race, of technology and capitalism, and it must cope with the spiritual frustrations and yearnings generated in the vast anonymity of global society. The great strength of democracy is its capacity for self-correction. Intelligent diagnosis and guidance are essential. "Perhaps no form of government," said Bryce, "needs great leaders so much as democracy." Yet even the greatest of democratic leaders lack the talent to cajole violent, retrograde, and intractable humankind into utopia. Still, with the failures of democracy in the twentieth century at the back of their minds, leaders in the twenty-first century may do a better job than we have done of making the world safe for democracy.

CHAPTER 7

THE INSCRUTABILITY
OF HISTORY

The life of the historian is a hazardous one. A perennial question assails us: What use is history anyway?

Hegel observed in the introduction to his *Philosophy of History*, "People and governments never have learned anything from history, or acted on principles deduced from it." Hegel exaggerated. For history is surely to the nation rather as memory is to the individual. As individuals deprived of memory become disoriented and lost, not knowing where they have been or where they are going, so a nation denied a conception of its past is disabled in dealing with its present and its future.

Yet history is subject to the same liabilities as memory—to the same whims, distortions, and corruptions that make memory self-serving, misleading, and unreliable. And the oracle of history, like the oracle of Delphi, is very often clouded and ambiguous.

The structure of President Bush's foreign policy, for example, rests squarely on the proposition that the intentions and capabilities of evil nations are readily predictable. Vice President Cheney and Secretary of Defense Rumsfeld evidently see themselves as "precogs" as in Steven Spielberg's film *Minority Report*. Precogs are psychically equipped to prevent crimes that are about to be committed. In the real world, preventive war depends on accurate intelligence, which is all too often unavailable, supplemented by dubious historical analogies—as in Iraq, where Cheney and Rumsfeld confidently predicted that the American invaders would be welcomed as liberators, not resented as occupiers, pelted with flowers, not bombs.

In this book I have tried to supply the historical background for current controversies in the hope that history might throw some light on choices that are ours, or at least our masters', to make.

As one who is by profession a historian and has been on occasion a government official, I have long been fascinated and perplexed by the interaction between history and public decision: fascinated because, by this process, past history becomes an active partner in the making of new history; perplexed because the role of history in this partnership remains both elusive and tricky.

It is elusive because, if one excludes charismatic politics—the politics of the prophet and the medicine man—one is bound to conclude that all thought which leads to decisions of public policy is in essence historical. Public decision in rational politics necessarily implies a guess about the future derived from the experience of the past. It implies an expectation, or at the very least a hope, that certain actions will produce tomorrow the same sort of results they produced yesterday. This guess about the future may be based on a comprehensive theory of historical change, as with the Marxists, or it may be based on an unstated and intuitive sense of the way things happen. But, whatever it is based on, it involves, explicitly or implicitly, a historical judgment.

And the problem is tricky because, when explicit historical judgments intervene, one immediately encounters a question which is, in the abstract, insoluble: Is the history invoked really the source of policies, or is it the source of arguments designed to vindicate policies adopted for other reasons? Moreover, even when history is in some sense the source of policies, the lessons of history are generally so ambiguous that the other reasons often determine the choice between alternative historical interpretations. Thus, in France, between the wars de Gaulle drew one set of conclusions from the First World War, and Pétain and Laval another. Yet one cannot, on the other hand, reduce the function of history in public policy to that of mere rationalization, for historical models acquire a life of their own. Once a statesman begins to identify the present with the past, he may in time be carried further than he intends by the bewitchment of analogy.

However hard it may be to define with precision the role of history in public policy, it is evident that this role must stand or fall on the success of history as a means of prediction—on the proposition that knowledge of yesterday provides guidance for tomorrow. This is a point, it should immediately be said, on which professional historians, on the whole, have few illusions among themselves. They privately regard history as its own reward; they study it for the intellectual and aesthetic fulfillment they find in the disciplined attempt to reconstruct the past and, perhaps, for the ironic aftertaste in the contemplation of man's heroism and folly, but for no more utilitarian reason. They understand better than outsiders that historical training confers no automatic wisdom in the realm of public affairs. Guizot, Bancroft, Macaulay, Thiers, Morley, Bryce, Theodore Roosevelt, Woodrow Wilson: one cannot say that their training as historians deeply influenced their practice as politicians; and the greatest of them—Roosevelt and Wilson—were harmed as politicians by exactly the moralism from which the study of history might have saved them. But then neither was a particularly good historian.

Yet historians, in spite of their candor within the fellowship, sometimes invoke arguments of a statelier sort in justifying themselves in society. Thus Sir Walter Raleigh: "We may gather out of History a policy no less wise than eternal; by the comparison and application of other men's fore-passed miseries with our own errors and ill-deservings." Or Edmund Burke: "In history, a great volume is unrolled for our instruction, drawing the materials of future wisdom from the past errors and infirmities of mankind." In what sense is this true? Why should history help us foresee the future? Because presumably history repeats itself enough to make possible a range of historical generalization; and because generalization, sufficiently multiplied and interlaced, can generate insight into the shape of things to come.

Many professional historians—perhaps most—reject the idea that generalization is the goal of history. We all respond, in Marc Bloch's phrase, to "the thrill of learning singular things." Indeed, it is the commitment to concrete reconstruction as against abstract generalization—to life as against laws—which distinguishes history from sociology. Yet, on the other hand, as Crane Brinton once put it, "the doctrine of the absolute uniqueness of events in history seems nonsense." Even historians who are skeptical of attempts to discern a final and systematic order in history acknowledge the existence of a variety of uniformities and recurrences. There can be no question that generalizations about the past, defective as they may be, are possible—and that they can strengthen the capacity of statesmen to deal with the future.

So historians have long since identified a life cycle of revolution which, if properly apprehended, might have spared us misconceptions about the Russian Revolution—first, about its goodwill, and later, when we abandoned belief in its goodwill, about the fixity and permanence of its fanatical purpose. Historical generalizations in a number of areas—the processes of economic development, for example, or the impact of industrialization and urbanization, or the effect of population growth, or the influence of climate or seapower or the frontier, or the circulation of political elites or entrepreneurial innovation—will enlarge the wisdom of the statesman, giving his responses to the crises of the moment perspective, depth, and an instinct for the direction and flow of events. Sometimes this wisdom may even lead to what Bloch called the "paradox of prevision"—to the point when men and women, sufficiently warned by historical extrapolation of horrid eventualities, may take action to avert them, which means that prevision may be destroyed by prevision.

The result is historical insight: that is, a sense of what is possible and probable in human affairs, derived from a feeling for the continuities and discontinuities of existence. This sense is comparable not to the mathematical equations of the physicist but to the diagnostic judgments of the doctor. It is this form of historical insight which has led in recent years to Bertrand de Jouvenel's *L'Art de la Conjecture* and to the stimulating intellectual exercise involved in the search for *futuribles*. But *futuribles* are speculative constructions of possible long-range futures, useful perhaps to those who may be presidents and prime ministers in 2050, hardly to their predecessors in 2004.

Still, every day around the planet great decisions are being made (or at least rationalized) in terms of short-run historical estimates. Marxism, of course, is sworn to a determinist view of the future, according to which fixed causes produce fixed effects and mankind is moving along a predestined path through predestined stages to a single predestined conclusion. For the Marxists, history has become a "positive model": it prescribes not only for the long but for the short run, not only strategy but tactics—the immediate policies to be favored, courses pursued, action taken. It is a tribute to the devotion of Marxists, if hardly to their intelligence, that they have remained so indefatigably loyal to their metaphysic in spite of the demonstrated limits of Marxism as a system of prediction.

For, if any thesis was central to the Marxist vision of history, it was that the process of modernization, of industrialization, of social and economic development, would infallibly carry every nation from feudalism through capitalism to communism: that the communist society was the inevitable culmination of the development process. Thus Marx contended that the more developed a country was, the more prepared it was for communism, and that communism in consequence must come first to the most industrialized nations. In fact, communism came only to nations in a relatively early stage of development, like Russia and China, and it came to such nations precisely as a means to modernization, not as a consequence of it. Instead of the climax of the development process, the end of the journey, communism is now revealed as a technique of social discipline which a few countries in early stages of development have adopted in the hope of speeding the pace of modernization. Instead of the ultimate destination toward which all societies are ineluctably moving, communism now appears an epiphenomenon of the transition from stagnation to development. Modernization, as it proceeds, evidently carries nations not toward Marx but away from Marx—and this was true of the Soviet Union itself.

History thus far has refuted the central proposition in Marx's system of prediction. It has also refuted important corollary theses—notably the idea that the free economic order could not possibly last. Far from obeying dogma and perishing of its own inner contradictions, free society in the developed world has rarely displayed more creativity and vitality. It cast as powerful a spell on the intellectuals and the youth of the communist world as the communist world cast on us during the Great Depression seventy years ago.

Why did Marx go wrong here? His forecast of the inevitable disintegration of free society was plausibly based on the laissez-faire capitalism of the mid-nineteenth century. This devil-take-the-hindmost economic order did very likely contain the seeds of its own destruction—especially in those tendencies, pronounced irreversible by Marx, toward an ever-widening gap between rich and poor (alleged to guarantee the ultimate impoverishment of the masses) and toward an ever-increasing frequency and severity of structural economic crisis (alleged to guarantee the progressive instability of the system). This may indeed be a salient example of the "paradox of prevision"; for the Marxist forecast unquestionably stimulated progressive democrats to begin the reform of classical capitalism through the invention of the affirmative state. "The more we condemn unadulterated Marxian Socialism," Theodore Roosevelt used to say, "the stouter should be our insistence on thoroughgoing social reforms." The combination of the affirmative state with the extraordinary success of the free economic order as an engine of production—a success which, contrary to laissez-faire dogma, government intervention increased rather than hampered—eventually thwarted the Marxist prophecy.

In the end, the Marxists were undone by Marxism. Ideology told them that those who owned the economy must own the state, and the state could therefore never act against their desires or interests. Yet fifteen years before *The Communist Manifesto*, an American president, Andrew Jackson, had already suggested that the state in a democratic society, far from being the instrument of the possessors, could well become the means by which those whom Jackson called the "humble members of society" might begin to redress the balance of social power against those whom Hamilton had called the "rich and well-born." Thus, in the twentieth-century developed world, the economic machine drowned the revolution in consumers' goods, while the affirmative state, with its policies of piecemeal intervention in the economy, brought about both a relative redistribution of wealth (defeating Marx's prediction of the immiseration of the poor) and a relative stabilization of the economy (defeating Marx's prediction of ever-deepening cyclical crisis). The last place to look for a Marxist victory is precisely the place where Marx said it would come first—in the most developed countries.

So the Marxist prophecy of a single obligatory destiny for humankind missed in both its parts: in its prediction of the irresistible breakdown of the free economy, and in its prediction of the irresistible triumph of communism as the fulfillment of the development process. In spite of many subsidiary insights and successes, Marxism must surely stand in our time as the spectacular flop of history as prophecy.

Yet the democratic world is hardly in a position to take too much satisfaction from the intellectual collapse of Marxism. It is true that our philosophical heritage—empirical, pragmatic, ironic, pluralistic, competitive—has happily inoculated us against rigid, all-encompassing, absolute systems of historical interpretation. But, though we may reject the view of history as metaphysically set and settled, we seem at times to embrace our own forms of historical fatalism, even if we invoke history less as theology than as analogy. This is only a marginal advantage. The argument by metaphor can generate a certitude almost as mischievous as the argument by determinism.

One thing that historical knowledge does rather well, and this is the cultivation of perspective. Dean Rusk, President Kennedy's secretary of state, used to tell the following story. During the Soviet blockade of Berlin in 1948, forebodings of a Third World War swept Washington. At a panicky staff meeting, a young assistant secretary exclaimed to Secretary of State George C. Marshall: "How in the world, Mr. Secretary, can you remain so calm during this appalling crisis?" Marshall replied serenely: "I've seen worse."

Americans have indeed seen worse. History, by putting crisis in perspective, supplies the antidote to every generation's illusion that its own problems are uniquely oppressive. Troubles impending always seem worse than troubles surmounted, but this does not prove that they really are. Perspective increases the sense that, with care and caution, firmness and intelligence, this crisis can be handled too.

For policymakers in a democracy, history generally appears as a "negative" rather than a "positive" model. It instructs us, not like Marxism, in the things we must do, but in the things we must *not* do—unless we wish to repeat the mistakes of our ancestors. The traumatic experience of the First World War thus dominated the diplomacy of the Second World War, at least as far as the United States was concerned. So the

American insistence on the doctrine of "Unconditional Surrender" in 1943 sprang from the belief that the failure to get unconditional surrender in 1918 had made possible the stab-in-the-back myth and guaranteed the revival of German nationalism. The American concern for the United Nations came from the conviction that the failure to join the League of Nations had opened the way to the Second World War. Franklin D. Roosevelt, a veteran of the Wilson administration, had learned from Wilson's mistakes. Not only did FDR insist on unconditional surrender, but he insisted on the launch of the United Nations while the war was still on, and he insisted on the inclusion of senators and Republicans in the delegation to the United Nations' founding conference. That is one reason why the 79th Congress overwhelmingly ratified the United Nations a quarter century after the 66th Congress rejected the League of Nations. Refuting Hegel, FDR used history with adroitness and wisdom.

The Second World War provided a new traumatic experience. In the years since, the consciousness of policymakers has been haunted by the Munich and Yalta analogies—the generalization, drawn from attempts to accommodate Adolf Hitler in 1938 and Joseph Stalin in 1945, that appeasement always assures new aggression. Of these analogies, Munich, as the more lucid in its pattern and the more emphatic in its consequence, has been the more powerful; Yalta figures rather as a complicated special case. I trust that a graduate student some day will write a doctoral essay on the influence of the Munich analogy on the subsequent history of the twentieth century. Perhaps in the end he or she will conclude that the multitude of errors committed in the name of "Munich" may exceed the original error of 1938.

Certainly Munich was a tragic mistake, and its lesson was that the appeasement of a highly wound up and heavily armed totalitarian state in the context of a relatively firm and articulated continental equilibrium of power was likely to upset the balance and make further aggression inevitable. But to conclude from this that all attempts to avert war by negotiation must always be "Munichs" goes beyond the evidence. No one understood this better than the greatest contemporary critic of Munich. A historian himself, Winston Churchill well appreciated the limits of historical analogy. So he defined the issue in his chapter on Munich in *The Gathering Storm*:

> It may be well here to set down some principles of morals and action which may be a guide in the future. No case of this kind can be judged apart from its circumstances. . . .
>
> Those who are prone to temperament and character to seek sharp and clear-cut solutions of difficult and obscure problems, who are ready to fight whenever some challenge comes from a foreign power, have not always been right. On the other hand, those whose inclination is to bow their heads, to seek patiently and faithfully for peaceful compromise, are not always wrong. On the contrary, in the majority of instances, they may be right, not only morally but from a practical standpoint. . . .
>
> How many wars have been precipitated by firebrands! How many misunderstandings which led to war could have been removed by temporising! How often

have countries fought cruel wars and then after a few years of peace found themselves not only friends but allies!

Sixteen years after Munich, when President Eisenhower invoked the Munich analogy to persuade the British to join the Americans in backing the French in Indochina, Churchill was unimpressed. He rejected Eisenhower's analogy, which did not, of course, prevent Churchill's successor as prime minister two years later from seeing Gamal Abdel Nasser and the Middle East in terms of 1938 and committing his nation to the Suez adventure. This time it was Eisenhower who rejected the Munich analogy. Such incidents illustrate the depressing persistence of the mentality which makes policy through stereotype, through historical generalization wrenched illegitimately out of the past and imposed mechanically on the future. Santayana's aphorism must be reversed: too often it is those who can remember the past who are condemned to repeat it.

"No case of this kind," Churchill said, "can be judged apart from its circumstances." I well remember President Kennedy after the Cuban missile crisis in 1962 privately expressing his fear that people would conclude from his victory that all we would have to do thereafter in dealing with the Communists was to be rough and they would collapse. The missile crisis, he pointed out, had three distinctive features: it occurred in a place where we enjoyed local conventional superiority, where Soviet national security was not directly engaged, and where the Russians lacked a case which they could convincingly sustain before the world. Things would be different, he said, if the situation were one where the communists had the local superiority, where their national security was directly engaged, and where they could persuade themselves and others they were in the right.

Kennedy, who, like Churchill, had the mind of a first-class historian, was without illusion about the infallibility of historical analogy. The point is not terribly complicated. Burke long ago warned against the practice of viewing an object "as it stands stripped of every relation, in all the nakedness and solitude of metaphysical abstraction. Circumstances (which with some gentlemen pass for nothing) give in reality to every political principle its distinguishing color and discriminating effect." Even Arnold Toynbee, the magician of historical analogy, has remarked that historians are

> never in a position to guarantee that the entities which we are bringing into comparison are properly comparable for the purpose of our investigation. . . . However far we may succeed in going in our search for sets of identical examples on either side, we shall never be able to prove that there is not some non-identical factor that we have overlooked, and this non-identical factor is not the decisive factor that accounts for the different outcomes in different cases of what has looked to us like an identical situation but may not have been this in truth.

Or, as Mark Twain put it, somewhat more vividly, in *Following the Equator*: "We should be careful to get out of an experience only the wisdom that is in it—and stop there; lest we be like the cat that sits down on a hot stove lid. She will never sit down on a hot stove lid again—and that is well; but also she will never sit down on a cold one."

One cannot doubt that the study of history makes people wiser. But it is indispensable to understand the limits of historical analogy. Most useful historical generalizations are statements about massive social and intellectual movements over a considerable period of time. They make large-scale, long-term prediction possible. But they do not justify small-scale, short-term prediction. For short-run prediction is the prediction of detail and, given the complex structure of social events, the difficulty of anticipating the intersection or collision of different events, and the irreducible mystery, if not invincible freedom, of individual decision, there are simply too many variables to warrant exact forecasts of the immediate future. History, in short, can answer questions, after a fashion, at long range. It cannot answer questions with confidence or certainty at short range. Alas, policymakers are rarely interested in the long run—"in the long run," as Keynes used to say, "we are all dead"—and the questions they put to history are thus most often the questions which history is least qualified to answer.

Far from offering a shortcut to clairvoyance, history teaches us that the future is full of surprises and outwits all our certitudes. For the study of history issues not in scientific precision nor in moral finality but in irony. If in 1940, anyone had predicted that before the end of the forties Germany and Japan would be well on the way to becoming close friends and allies of Britain and the United States, he would have been considered mad. If in 1950, as the Russians and

Chinese were signing their thirty-year pact of amity and alliance, anyone predicted that by the end of the fifties they would be at each other's throats, he too would have been considered mad. The chastening fact is that many of the pivotal events of our age were unforeseen: from the Nazi-Soviet pact and the Tito-Stalin quarrel of years ago to such events in today's newspapers as 9/11 and Abu Ghraib.

Occasionally one reads in the American press that leading political figures in Washington are shaping their actions today by calculations with regard to the Democratic presidential nomination in 2008. I am sure that the persons mentioned in such stories are themselves under no delusion about the hopelessness of such an undertaking. "In politics," Harold Wilson used to say, "a week is a very long time." The year 2008 is as far away from 2004 as 2000 is, and no one reflecting on the unpredictability of the last four years in the United States could sensibly suppose that the next four are going to be any more predictable. I have often thought that a futurist trying to forecast the next three American presidents in early 1940 would hardly have named as the first president after Franklin D. Roosevelt an obscure back-bench senator from Missouri, anticipating defeat by the governor of his state in the Democratic primaries; as the second, an unknown lieutenant colonel in the United States Army; and, as the third, a kid still in college. Yet that sequence began to unfold in less time than between 2003 and 2008.

The salient fact about the historical process, so far as the short run is concerned, is its inscrutability. A few years back, there was the question of Communist China, then the militantly ideological state of Chairman Mao. The argument was heard that we must have a showdown with Red China before it gets the bomb. Who could possibly predict with assurance that the Chinese Revolution would undertake the conquest of the world? The study of revolution has shown us that the emotional and doctrinal pitch of revolutions waxes and wanes; that, while revolutions at first may devour their children, in the end the children sometimes devour the revolutions; that even totalitarian revolutions fail at total mass indoctrination; that a successful revolution begins to develop a stake in the status quo; that post-revolutionary generations have their own identities and aspirations; that the possession of a major nuclear arsenal has thus far had a sobering effect on the possessor; that nations follow their historic interests rather more faithfully than they do their ideologies; and that there is no greater error than to try and deduce the policy of the future from the rhetoric of the present.

Nor does the example of Hitler and *Mein Kampf* change this. Hitler was indeed the man on the bicycle; he had to keep moving. The Nazi revolution never got beyond the first messianic phase; its nature condemned it to *Götterdämmerung*. We must not forget that the Chinese regime has already lasted nearly half a century longer than the whole life of the Third Reich. And as we have seen in the case of the Soviet Union, the permutation and erosion of time and national interest undermined what were once thought to be final motives and permanent objectives. With an equation so overflowing with variables, how can anyone forecast today the behavior of China twenty years from now?

The idea was prevalent forty years ago that the future of East Asia depended on the outcome of the civil war in Vietnam. Thirty years ago the Communists won that war. Today we have normal relations with the Communist regime, and East Asia is much the same. We were eyeless in Vietnam too, rushing to set things straight while bereft of historic experience; "didn't know the territory," to quote *The Music Man*.

Ignorance is no pathway to success; and Iraq seems likely to end as a repetition of Vietnam. It is improbable that Cheney and Rumsfeld are going to overcome deep-rooted religious and cultural obstacles and transform the land they have impetuously invaded into a Jeffersonian democracy. Even in parts of the world like Latin America where we have had historic experience, we not infrequently get things wrong.

History too often equips presidents with good rather than real reasons. This is not an argument against the knowledge of history: it is an argument against the superficial knowledge of history. The single analogy is never enough to penetrate a process so cunningly compounded not only of necessity but of contingency, fortuity, ignorance, stupidity, and chance.

The statesman who is surest that he can divine the will of the Almighty most urgently invites his own retribution. The theologian Reinhold Niebuhr warned against "the depth of evil to which individuals and communities may sink, particularly when they try to play the role of God to history." "The hardest strokes of heaven," the historian Herbert Butterfield has written, "fall in history upon those who imagine that they can control things in a sovereign manner, playing providence not only for themselves but for the far future—reaching out into the future with the wrong kind of farsightedness, and gambling on a lot of risky calculations in which there must never be a single mistake."

The only antidote to a shallow knowledge of history is a deeper knowledge, the knowledge which produces not dogmatic certitude but diagnostic skill, not clairvoyance but insight. It offers the statesman a sense, at once, of short-run variables and long-run tendencies, and an instinct for the complexity of their intermingling, including the understanding that (as Rousseau once put it) "the ability to foresee that some things cannot be foreseen is a very necessary quality." Indeed, half the wisdom of statecraft, to borrow a phrase from Richard Goodwin of the JFK circle, is "to leave as many options open as possible and decide as little as possible. . . . Since almost all important policy judgments are speculative, you must avoid risking too much on the conviction you are right."

Of course keeping too many options open too long may paralyze the lobe of decision and lose the game. There *does* come a time when accommodation turns into appeasement. This is the other half of the wisdom of statecraft: to accept the chronic obscurity of events without yielding, in Lincoln's words, firmness in the right as God gives us to see the right. In deciding when to decide, the criterion must be the human consequences—the results for people, not for doctrine.

Randolph Churchill's life of his father reproduces an extraordinary letter written seventy years ago by the young Winston Churchill to a New York politician of the time,

Bourke Cockran. "The duty of government," Churchill said, "is to be first of all practical. I am for makeshifts and expediency. I would like to make the people who live on this world at the same time as I do better fed and happier generally. If incidentally I benefit posterity—so much the better—but I would not sacrifice my own generation to a principle however high or a truth however great."

Such an approach may seem too modest, even perhaps too cynical, for these messianic statesmen whose self-righteousness bids fair to wreck our age. Most of these confident moralists have been high priests of one or another dogmatic faith; and all have been prepared in the best conscience and in the name of history to sacrifice their generations on the altars of their own metaphors. It can only be said that, whether they see history as ideology or as analogy, they see it wrong. Far from unveiling the secret of things to come, history bestows a different gift: it makes us—or should make us—understand the extreme difficulty, the intellectual peril, the moral arrogance of supposing that the future will yield itself so easily to us.

"I returned," Ecclesiastes reminds us, "and saw under the sun that the race is not to the swift, nor the battle to the strong, neither yet bread to the wise nor riches to men of understanding, but time and chance happeneth to them all." The Old Testament carries the case against historical generalization to the extreme. But without going so far, we can agree that history should lead statesmen to a profound and humbling sense of human frailty—to a recognition of the fact, so insistently demonstrated by experience and so tragically destructive of our most cherished certitudes, that the possibilities of history are far richer and more various than the human intellect is likely to conceive. This, and the final perception that while the tragedy of history implicates us all in the common plight of humanity, we are never relieved, despite the limits of our knowledge and the darkness of our understanding, from the necessity of meeting our obligations.

CHAPTER 8

HOLY WARS

Religion and the American Presidency

"I'm an atheist, thank God!"   —Luis Buñuel

"A fanatic is a man that does what he thinks th' Lord
wud do if He only knew th' facts in th' case."
          —Mr. Dooley [Finley Peter Dunne]

George W. Bush is the most aggressively religious
president in American history. Despite press conference protestations that he regards religion as a personal and private matter, he is endeavoring to remold the
American presidency, hitherto a secular office, into a "faith-
based" presidency, unknown to past presidents, unknown to
the Constitution. President Bush's new conception owes
much to the zeal of the convert. Also it owes much to his will
and skill as a political leader.

He achieved a drastic revolution in replacing contain-
ment/deterrence with preventive war as the basis of foreign
policy. And in seeking to replace a secular presidency by a

faith-based presidency he is projecting an equally drastic revolution in domestic policy. In both cases, he made the revolutions invisible. Instead of setting off vehement argument
over 180-degree reversals in national policy, President Bush,
through political dexterity combined with political determination, has succeeded thus far in escaping debate. In both
cases, he was aided by the timorous media, which failed to
clarify the meaning of the reversals and failed to give anything like equal time to the opposition. And he was aided by
the Democratic party's fear of seeming anti-patriotic in challenging Bush's preventive-war doctrine and of seeming anti-
religious in challenging 'people of faith.'

In President Bush's mind, patriotism and faith united in
the decision to invade Iraq. Some say that he is fighting a holy
war predicated on his religious convictions. According to the
highly sympathetic book by Peter and Rochelle Schweitzer,
The Bushes: Portrait of a Dynasty, a family member said,
"George sees this as a religious war. His view of this is that
they are trying to kill the Christians. And we Christians will
strike back with more force and more ferocity than they will
ever know."

Our president's exchange with Bob Woodward, referred to
in chapter 2, throws more light on the U.S. decision to launch
a preventive war against Iraq. A senior aide commented to
Woodward that the president "really believes that he was
placed there to do this as part of a divine plan." Woodward
asks President Bush whether he consulted with his father, the
elder President Bush, who a few years before had dealt effi-
ciently with the Iraqi invasion of Kuwait. "He is the wrong

father to appeal to in terms of strength," Bush replies. "There is a higher father that I appeal to." (The higher father's message was evidently murky. Pope John Paul II, who had his own private line to the Almighty, stoutly opposed the Iraq War.)

George Bush's reliance on religion in his decision to go to war against Iraq raises the interesting question of the role of religion in the American presidency. The United States was founded on the idea of human rights, regardless of how imperfectly the idea was embodied in the slave-owning commonwealth. Orators like to trace the idea to religious sources, especially to the so-called Judeo-Christian tradition. In fact, the great religious ages were notable for their indifference to human rights in the contemporary sense—not only their acquiescence in poverty, inequality, and oppression but their enthusiastic justification of slavery, persecution, torture, and assassination.

Christianity in particular assigned to human misery an honored and indispensable role in the grand drama of salvation. From the religious perspective, nothing that took place on earth mattered in comparison with what must take place hereafter. The trials visited on humankind in this world were ordained by the Almighty in order to test sinful mortals. The world was but an inn at which humans spent a night on their voyage to eternity, so what difference could it make if the food were disgusting or the innkeeper a brute? Till the end of the eighteenth century, torture was normal investigative procedure in the Catholic Church as well as in most secular nations (and in Salem, Massachusetts).

Human rights—roughly, the idea that all individuals everywhere are entitled to life, liberty, and the pursuit of happiness on this earth—is a modern proposition, hardly more than two centuries old. No doubt the idea of human rights had classical antecedents among, for example, the Stoics. But humanitarianism—the notion that human rights have immediate, concrete, and universal application within history—is the product of the Enlightenment. The Americans crystallized the revolutionary new doctrine by coming up with the phrase "the pursuit of happiness." The phrase happily combined two ideas—not only the right to seek happiness but the right to obtain happiness. As John Adams said, "The happiness of society is the end of government."

Tocqueville persuasively attributed the humanitarian ethic to the rise of the idea of equality—equality before the law, leading on to equal treatment of other equal individuals. In aristocratic societies, he wrote in *Democracy in America*, the upper caste believed that its inferiors hardly "belong to the same race." When medieval chroniclers "relate the tragic end of a noble, their grief flows apace, whereas they tell you at a breath and without wincing of massacres and tortures inflicted on the common sort." Tocqueville recalled the "cruel jocularity" with which the delightful Madame de Sévigné, one of the most civilized women of the seventeenth century, described the breaking on a wheel of an itinerant fiddler "for getting up a dance and stealing some stamped paper." It would be wrong, Tocqueville thought, to suppose that Madame de Sévigné was inhuman or sadistic. Rather, she "had no clear notion of suffering in anyone who was not a person of quality."

The Enlightenment changed all that. Once people began seeing each other as more or less equal, there arose a mood of what Tocqueville called "general compassion." Equality bred "sympathy," which Dr. Johnson defined as "the consciousness that we have the same nature with the sufferer, that we are in danger of the same distresses." This was a novel thought, and the cult of sympathy made it increasingly difficult to dismiss the less fortunate as creatures of some lower race—unless, of course, they were legally unequal, like black slaves in the United States. It was the Enlightenment, not the "Judeo-Christian tradition" (not yet invented), that sponsored the decline of religious persecution, the rise of tolerance, the rejection of torture and of public executions, the new attention to the enslaved, the poor, and the mad.

Since religion had customarily ordained hierarchy and inequality, early human rights advocacy, as with Voltaire and later in the French Revolution, had a markedly anti-clerical cast. Only as religion itself began to succumb to the humanitarian ethic and to see the Kingdom of God as attainable within history could the claim be made that the "Judeo-Christian tradition" commanded the pursuit of happiness in this world. The basic human rights documents—the American Declaration of Independence and the Constitution, the French Declaration of the Rights of Man—were written by political, not by religious, leaders.

Certainly the founders of the American republic were children of the Enlightenment. They did not even mention God in their (our) Constitution. The only allusion to religion in the original text beyond the date ("in the year of our

Lord") came in Article VI: "no religious Test shall ever be required as a Qualification to any Office or public trust under the United States." Benjamin Franklin, the oldest and wisest of the lot, expressed doubts about the divinity of Christ a couple of months before his own death. Characteristically, Franklin made a joke out of it: "Though it is a question I do not ever dogmatize upon, having never studied it, and think it needless to busy myself with it now when I expect soon an opportunity of knowing the truth with much less trouble."

Persons of faith regarded our early presidents as inadequately devout. George Washington was a nominal Virginia Episcopalian who rarely stayed for communion and issued no religious statement on his deathbed. John Adams was a Massachusetts Unitarian, which trinitarians abhorred as heresy. Thomas Jefferson, denounced by people of faith as an atheist, was actually a deist who detested the priesthood and produced an expurgated version of the New Testament minus the miracles. James Madison, another nominal Virginia Episcopalian, was the architect of the Virginia Statute of Religious Freedom; he said, "Religion flourishes in greater purity, without than with the aid of Government." James Monroe was still another Virginia Episcopalian. John Quincy Adams was another Massachusetts Unitarian.

The case of George Washington, the father of his country, is revealing. His military orders during the War for Independence and during his presidency were filled with highly generalized invocations to Divine Providence or the Supreme Ruler of Nations (he rarely referred to God) but without any theological specifics or detail. With superb tact and, it must be said, with superb wisdom he embodied a pluralist conception which he applied not only to Protestant denominations but also to Catholics and Jews; even to Mohammedans, in the Treaty of Tripoli, whose Article XI affirms: "As the Government of the United States is not in any sense founded on the Christian religion. . . ."

This treaty was signed on November 4, 1796, when Washington was president (and Timothy Pickering, a high Federalist, was secretary of state). It was negotiated by the epic poet and spirited adventurer Joel Barlow, who was appointed consul to Algiers and charged with securing the release of American prisoners captured by Barbary pirates. President Washington signed Article XI, and the Senate ratified the treaty unanimously on June 10, 1797, no senator objecting to the statement that the republic was not founded on the Christian religion.

The election of Jefferson in 1800 brought to the White House the man who people of faith regarded as the primary enemy. Alexander Hamilton in his last pessimistic years pronounced the Constitution a "frail and worthless fabric" and in 1802 offered a "Christian Constitutional Society" as a remedy. Hamilton's project got nowhere, even among Federalists. Denominational issues appeared to be removed from politics.

In 1815 Lyman Beecher, emerging as a Presbyterian leader, proposed that a religious instructor be set up for every thousand persons—a proposal that provoked Jefferson into a diatribe against "the pious whining, the hypocritical canting, lying & slandering" of what he called the "priesthood." But the Sabbatarian controversy of the 1820s revived the evangelical community as a pressure group in American politics.

In 1810 a Jeffersonian Congress had passed a law requiring Sunday postal service. The issue of Sunday mails affronted the pious, much as same-sex marriage affronts the pious today. The Sabbath, the devout felt, should be reserved for sermonizing and praying; government should not encourage secular activities. In 1827 the Reverend Ezra Stiles Ely called for "a Christian party in politics." The next year evangelicals formed a General Union for Promoting the Observance of the Christian Sabbath. By the presidency of Andrew Jackson in 1829, the evangelicals were well organized as a political force. The Second Great Awakening was well under way.

This roused the Jacksonians. Pay no attention, by the way, to the portrayal of the Jacksonians by Walter Russell Mead and Anatol Lieven as fundamentalists. Quite the contrary; the freethinkers of the time were Jacksonians. "Wherever you find a bitter, blasphemous Atheist and an enemy of Marriage, Morality, and Social Order," said the great Whig editor Horace Greeley in the 1840 presidential election, "there you may be certain of one vote for Van Buren." Above all, Colonel Richard M. Johnson of Kentucky, putative killer of Tecumseh and leader in the fight to abolish imprisonment for debt, was strategically placed as chairman of the Senate Post Office Committee. In 1828 Johnson had submitted a report declaring that it was unconstitutional for the national government to promote Sabbath observance by outlawing Sunday mail services. "Our Government," Johnson said, "is a civil, and not a religious, institution." Pointing out that some Americans celebrated Sabbath on Saturday rather than Sunday, Johnson said, "The Constitution regards the conscience of the Jew as sacred as that of the Christian."

Such views angered the evangelical sects, who threatened divine punishment on behalf of Providence. Lyman Beecher's organ, *The Spirit of the Pilgrims*, observed menacingly, "Whoever contended with his Maker and prospered? Does He not hold at his disposal all the sources of national prosperity?" But the ungodly ignored the warning, and so did Americans in general. Colonel Johnson's report was printed on satin and hung in parlors, offices, and barrooms over the land.

The very defeat of the evangelical campaign against the Sunday mails strengthened the conviction that people of faith must enter politics to rescue the republic from infidelity. Two issues in Jackson's first term confirmed that conviction. President Jackson rejected a clerical appeal that he proclaim a national day of fasting and prayer in order to combat a cholera epidemic. The second issue was Jackson's refusal to intervene in the case of the Georgia missionaries who violated a state law and remained in prison for over a year. Jackson rewarded Colonel Johnson by making him the running mate of his chosen successor Martin Van Buren—this despite the technical handicap in those benighted days of Vice President Johnson's living openly with and having daughters by a black woman.

The Jacksonian theory of the relations of church and state did not imply a weak personal faith. Old Hickory himself was a regular churchgoer, though not a communicant till 1839.

James K. Polk—Young Hickory—was faithful in his Sunday observance. But they both firmly opposed the political aspirations of religion. Polk, a Presbyterian himself, told a Presbyterian minister who mixed religion and politics "that, thank God, under our constitution there was no connection between Church and State, and that in my action as President of the U.S. I recognized no distinction of creeds in my appointments to office." He had met no one in these first two years of his administration, Polk later wrote, who so disgusted him. "I have a great veneration and regard for Religion & sincere piety, but a hypocrite or a bigotted fanatic without reason I cannot bear."

In the nineteenth century, all presidents routinely invoked God and solicited His blessing. But religion did not occupy a major presence in their lives, with the possible exception of Lincoln—and Lincoln rejected the "Christian Amendment" aimed at writing "Almighty God" and "Lord Jesus Christ" into the Constitution. Agitation for the Christian Amendment kept up for a decade after the Civil War until the House Judiciary Committee declared it inexpedient "to put anything into the Constitution . . . which might be construed to be a reference to any religious creed." Nor did nineteenth-century presidents exploit their religion for political benefit. "I would rather be defeated," said James A. Garfield, "than make Capital out of my Religion."

Nor was there any great popular demand that politicians should be men of faith (so long as they were not communicants of the party of Rum, Romanism and Rebellion). In 1876 James G. Blaine, a candidate for the Republican presidential nomination, selected Colonel Robert G. Ingersoll, a famed orator but a notorious scoffer at religion, to deliver the nominating speech. "The Great Agnostic" did so with wit, eloquence, and style. A twenty-first-century equivalent of Colonel Ingersoll would be blacklisted by Karl Rove, President Bush's political wizard, and hissed off the platform at Republican conventions.

Religion of course affected the climate of opinion and helped shape the foundations of democracy. Its essential role was its quickening power in the individual soul; its essential function was to lead the soul to salvation. But in a democracy, religious beliefs were bound to have political implications. Religion gave moral energy to the abolitionist movement and was largely responsible for its impact. It should not be forgotten, however, that religion also lent moral force to the defense of slavery. Pro-slavery clerics felt they had the better of the biblical argument; after all, Christ had never condemned slavery. At the turn of the twentieth century, the Social Gospel of Walter Rauschenbusch and Washington Gladden helped create and extend the humanitarian mood that galvanized the Progressive era.

There have been presidents of ardent religious faith in the twentieth century. Woodrow Wilson had no doubt that God had anointed the United States—and himself—for the salvation of suffering humanity. Jimmy Carter, like the second George Bush, had been born again. Ronald Reagan, though not much of a churchgoer, persuaded the evangelicals that he was one of them. Bill Clinton was never more inspired than in a church, especially a black church. All embraced religion as a personal, private faith. But neither Wilson nor Carter nor Reagan nor Clinton applied religious tests to public policy, nor did they rely on religious leaders and churches to mobilize voters on their behalf.

These two standards are challenged by our forty-third president, George W. Bush. His conception of a faith-based presidency would have startled the founding fathers. Is that conception a good thing for democracy? Is that a good thing indeed for religion?

It certainly is a good thing personally for President Bush. He would not be president today had not a vivid religious experience charged his life with new meaning, direction, and discipline. His first forty years had been a wasteland of drift, aimlessness, buffoonery, business failures, and excessive drinking. Redemption and transformation through commitment to Jesus made him "born again" into a self-confident man and a considerable leader.

His parents are conventional Episcopalians, and for a while young George conventionally attended the Presbyterian church in Midland, Texas. Marriage and Laura involved him with the Methodists. But he missed something, as he said, "on the inside." In the summer of 1985, while visiting his parents in Kennebunkport, George W. took his famous walk along the rugged Maine shore with Billy Graham. "Are you right with God?" Graham asked. "No," Bush answered, "but I want to be."

"That weekend," Bush later recalled, "my faith took on new meaning. It was the beginning of a new walk where I would recommit my heart to Jesus Christ." He gave up drinking, smoking, and tobacco-chewing. In Midland, he joined a men's community Bible study group devoted to intensive reading of scripture. When his father ran for president in 1988, young George served as an informal liaison with the religious right. Turning to politics, he was elected governor of Texas. By this time he was a regular reader of the Bible and enjoyed a personal relation with his savior.

Reelected governor, he decided in 1999 to run for president. Asked on television about his favorite philosopher, he replied, "Christ, because he changed my heart." He said to members of the Southern Baptist Convention, "I believe that God wants me to be president." To a Houston minister, he said, "I believe I am called to run for the presidency." These statements assumed a sort of validity when the Almighty, apparently working through the Supreme Court of the United States, delivered the White House to George W. Bush in 2000. The new president was a great believer in the power of prayer. At a White House reception he said, "Our country has been delivered from many serious evils and wrongs because of that prayer."

President Bush's conversion experience was undoubtedly authentic. But his faith also provides political benefits. "There's no question that the president's faith is real, genuine," said Doug Wead, an Assemblies of God evangelist, once one of Bush's close religious friends, "and there's no question that it's calculated." The rise of Protestant evangelicals as a political force has restructured American politics, and President Bush is taking full advantage of the millennial fervor.

When I was young, Protestant evangelicals were a disdained minority, made sport of by H. L. Mencken as inhabitants of the Bible Belt. Fundamentalists were (are) true believers in the inerrancy of scriptures, including Genesis creationism. John T. Scopes, a high school teacher in Dayton, Tennessee, had violated a state law banning the teaching of Darwinian evolution, and the Scopes case in 1925 generally held fundamentalists up to ridicule. Two years later Sinclair Lewis wrote *Elmer Gantry*, dedicated to Mencken and fixing the stereotype of con-man evangelists. One wonders whether two powerful 1960 films, *Inherit the Wind* (Stanley Kramer) and *Elmer Gantry* (Richard Brooks), would be made in today's evangelical piety.

Born-again fundamentalists could be relied upon in those forgotten days to be anti-Catholic and anti-Semitic. They listened to Tom Watson, Tom Heflin, Theodore (The Man) Bilbo, John Rankin, Gene Tallmadge, and led the bitter campaigns against Al Smith in 1928 and John F. Kennedy in 1960. They had lynched Leo Frank in Georgia in 1915. But anti-Catholicism and anti-Semitism kept fundamentalism a small, isolated, despised sect of fanatics. Cooler heads, like Ralph Reed, eventually prevailed, and evangelicals dumped their offensive doctrines. In recent years the Protestant right (as explained in chapter 2) has forged an alliance with right-wing Catholics over abortion and with right-wing Jews over the Holy Land. Such alliances give fundamentalists a measure of political respectability and influence.

Religious statistics are notoriously unreliable, but it may be, as the Pew Center for the People and the Press asserts, that evangelicals now outnumber mainline Protestants; they certainly outshout them. In the late 1980s, according to the Pew Center, 41 percent of Protestants identified themselves as "born-again or evangelical." Today, 54 percent of Protestants identify themselves that way. Evangelicals make up to 30 percent of the population, and with their allies among right wing Catholics and Jews, make up close to 40 percent of the electorate.

Confronting the 2004 election, Karl Rove worried about evangelical voters. The elder George Bush had alienated the religious right—one reason for his defeat in 1992—and the younger George Bush was determined not to repeat his father's mistake. Rove estimated that 4 million of their born-again brethren had not voted in 2000. In July 2004, the Bush campaign, the *New York Times* reported, "has laid out a brisk schedule for legions of Christian supporters to help enlist 'conservative churches' and their members, including sending church directories to the campaign, according to a Bush campaign document."

President Bush himself told a White House conference of religious organizations that the federal government had given more than $1 billion in 2003 to faith-based groups. In August 2004, as the presidential contest grew more heated, the *Times* ran a story under the headline CHURCHES SEE AN ELECTION ROLE AND SPREAD THE WORD ON BUSH. The *Wall Street Journal* described the weekly conference call between the White House and right-wing Christian leaders. When the president addressed the Southern Baptist Convention, a chorus line of ministers pledged to call for his re-election.

The Rove strategy proved effective in mobilizing religious voters, but it was a far cry from the attitude of such nineteenth-century presidents as Polk and Garfield. Bush and his faith-based presidency justified the rebuke by Ron Reagan, who said at his father's funeral that President Reagan had "never made the fatal mistake of so many politicians—wearing his faith on his sleeve to gain political advantage."

Bush's is the first faith-based administration in the history of the United States. John Ashcroft, the former U.S. attorney general in the first term, is a Pentecostalist and held prayer meetings in his office. Michael Gerson, Bush's primary speechwriter in the first term (and an eloquent speechwriter he is), is an evangelical Christian who majored in theology at Wheaton College. David Frum, a quondam speechwriter, reports that the first words he heard in the Bush White House were "Missed you at Bible study." A senior White House official told David Aikman, author of an admiring Bush biography, *A Man of Faith: The Spiritual Journey of George W. Bush*, about seven separate Bible study and prayer groups meeting every week in the White House, involving some 200 out of 500 staffers—all presumably meeting on taxpayers' time. Aikman quotes a BBC correspondent: "It's not uncommon to see White House functionaries hurrying down corridors carrying Bibles."

Bush's re-election in 2004 consolidated the religious right's occupation of Washington. "It's what Ralph Reed dreamed of, and now it's finally here," read a dispatch in *The Washington Post* in March 2005. ". . . This year evangelicals in public office have finally become so numerous that they've blended in to the permanent Washington backdrop, a new establishment that has absorbed the local habits and mores.

Nearly every third congressional office stocks an ambitious Christian leader who calls himself 'evangelical.' " "One of the biggest changes in my lifetime," said Bill Moyers, "is that the delusional is no longer marginal. It has come in from the fringe, to sit in the seat of power in the Oval Office and in Congress. For the first time in our history, ideology and theology hold a monopoly of power in Washington."

Some Republicans are uncomfortable with the political exploitation of religion. An exasperated Republican congressman from Connecticut, Christopher Shays, observes, "This Republican party of Lincoln has become a party of theocracy." ABC's George Stephanopoulos posed a question to Governor Arnold Schwarzenegger of California: "You're a Catholic. How do you reconcile your political positions on abortion, on gay rights, on the death penalty? They're opposed to the positions of the Catholic church." Schwarzenegger replied, "It's easy. . . . I never have one sleepless night over it. . . . I'm representing the people of California. The people of California all of them are not Catholics so, therefore, I do not bring my religion into this whole thing. As a matter of fact, religion should have no effect on politics. . . . If you make a decision, it should not be based on your religious beliefs. It should be based on how can you represent the people of California the best possible way? We have Jews, we have Christians and we have Hindus. We have Buddhists. . . . There's some 140 religions in this state. I have to represent all of them." One hundred forty religions?—but then the state is California. Even William F. Buckley, Jr., appears concerned over evangelicals in power: "Conservatives will keep our eyes on President Bush, and stop him before he campaigns for compulsory baptism."

Bush's first executive order was to set up in the White House the Office of Faith-Based and Community Initiatives. The idea behind this unprecedented office was to steer federal funds into religious welfare organizations. Sub-offices were established in seven agencies, including the Departments of Justice, Labor, Agriculture, and Health and Human Services. "I welcome faith," President Bush said, "to solve the nation's deepest problems." "I don't think there's any question," says Richard Land of the Southern Baptist Convention, "that his faith was absolutely determinative in his decision making." The Bush administration does have an evident preference for faith-based programs, as two newspaper headlines in May 2005 illustrate: "TWO FRONTS IN THE WAR ON POVERTY; WHILE BUSH SEEKS MORE AID FOR CHURCH GROUPS, OTHER PROGRAMS FACE AN UNCERTAIN FUTURE," *Washington Post*; "HISPANIC GROUP THRIVES ON FAITH AND FEDERAL AID: BUSH INITIATIVE HELPS A MINISTER INCREASE HIS INFLUENCE," *New York Times*. The Bush administration gave more than $2 billion to faith-based organizations in 2004, the year of the presidential election.

Bush is unique among presidents in his extensive application of religious tests to secular problems. That is why 48 American Nobel laureates called for a regime change in Washington in the 2004 election and the recent wave of critical reports by the National Academy of Sciences. And this explains Bush's threat to veto a bill passed by the House of Representatives promoting embryonic stem-cell research—

an opposition that so distresses Nancy Reagan. Stem-cell research promises to expedite cures for diabetes, Alzheimer's, Parkinson's, AIDS, and other diseases. But evangelicals are against it, and so is George Bush. (Tony Blair is for it, on the ground that, as a member of his cabinet said, "The UK is the place to come to carry out research in leading-edge areas, such as stem cell research.")

The ideology of the religious right surely explains Bush's call for a constitutional amendment to ban same-sex marriage. Had the Supreme Court upheld the decision of the Ninth Circuit to delete "under God" from the pledge of allegiance, Bush doubtless would have proposed another constitutional amendment.

During the 2000 election, Bush allowed that he thought schools should teach creationism as well as evolution. Nineteen state legislatures are arguing about legislative proposals that prefer Genesis to Darwin. According to the National Science Teachers Association, a poll of more than a thousand science teachers shows that 30 percent felt pressure to include creationism in their courses. True believers in the Bible Belt so harass teachers that, as one high school biology teacher said, she simply ignored evolution because she knew she'd get into trouble with the principal if word got about that she was teaching it. The potent fundamentalist crusade for creationism in public schools eighty years later would leave H. L. Mencken incredulous and William Jennings Bryan exultant.

Then there is the curious episode of the evangelical attempt to take over the Air Force Academy, a government institution on the model of West Point and Annapolis. The academy is located in Colorado Springs, described by Jeff Sharlet in *Harper's* as "home to the greatest concentration of fundamentalist Christian activist groups in American history." The infection spread to the academy which, according to the Associated Press, "is scrambling to address complaints that evangelical Christians wield so much influence . . . that religious harassment has become pervasive." The second in command at the academy, a born-again general, was accused of propagating his evangelical faith through speeches and memoranda. There were fifty-five complaints over four years. A Jewish cadet was told, for example, that the Holocaust was punishment for the Jewish race because Jews had killed Jesus.

Finally, after four years, a team from the Yale Divinity School investigated the academy and endorsed the complaints. The chief chaplain asked a woman chaplain to denounce the Yale report. She refused, saying she agreed with the report. A few weeks later she received orders to go to Okinawa where she can be assigned to Iraq or Afghanistan. Forty-seven members of Congress have asked the acting secretary of the air force what in the world is going on in the Air Force Academy—in addition to rapes of female cadets, the subject of prior investigations. The superintendent, a lieutenant general, was asked how long it would take to restore religious tolerance to the Academy. He replied, "If everything goes well, it's probably going to take six years to fix it." Meanwhile the scandal of evangelical proselytizing at a government institution and at taxpayers' expense has generated a vast indifference on the part of the media, with one or two exceptions.

Evangelicals impose their faith on the unwilling, as at the Air Force Academy. The National Park Service, yielding to evangelical pressure, sells a creationist book explaining that Noah's flood produced the Grand Canyon. "At the Riverview Community Bank in Otsego, Minn.," the *New York Times Magazine* reported, "the employees pray with customers and proselytize." Local school and library boards are particularly vulnerable to moralistic zealots—the flaw in the cult of communitarianism. Evangelical Christians try to drive out of libraries and bookshops works of which they disapprove; Harry Potter and *The da Vinci Code* are favorite targets. And they rush to buy, and perhaps to believe, the Rapture literature, especially the twelve-volume best-selling Left Behind series. Tim Lahaye and Jerry Jenkins portray with a certain relish the second coming of Jesus to the Holy Land and the fate of clueless people led by the Antichrist, who turns out to be secretary-general of the United Nations: "Jesus merely raised one hand a few inches and . . . they tumbled in, howling and screeching." "Gosh, what an uplifting scene!" exclaims Nicholas D. Kristof of the *New York Times* (satirically).

Theological restrictions on scientific inquiry and humanitarian action are especially burdensome on women. Bush's rigid opposition to abortion colors every government decision that affects family planning. In July 2004, the administration for the third year withheld $34 million from the United Nations Population Fund on the ground that, while the UN agency does not provide for abortion, it cooperates with Chinese programs that may involve abortion. The fund cutoff punishes poor women around the world.

The tragedy of September 11 deepened Bush's relationship with his creator. As noted in chapter 2, the president radiates a calm but disquieting certitude on questions of life and death. His faith-based presidency banishes doubt and encourages absolutism: either you're for us or for the terrorists. He has remade himself through redemption and transformation, and he may well regard it as his God-given destiny to redeem and transform the Middle East. He sees his administration as agents selected by the Almighty to combat evil and establish virtue. (Of course, Osama bin Laden thinks the same way.)

"In the argument over slavery in the 1850s, Lincoln did not ordinarily rest his argument on religious grounds," William Lee Miller writes in his ethical biography, *Lincoln's Virtues*. " . . . The authoritative criterion that Lincoln *did* use was an earthbound one: the Declaration of Independence." Of all our American presidents, Lincoln had the most acute religious insight. Though not enrolled in any denomination, he brooded over the infinite mystery of the Almighty. He was intensely aware of the unfathomable distance between the Supreme Being and erring mortals. He would have agreed with Hawthorne that to claim knowledge of the divine will and purpose was the unpardonable sin. He would have rejoiced in Mr. Dooley's definition of a fanatic. The most dangerous people in the world are those who convince themselves that they execute the will of the Almighty.

During the Civil War, as Isaac Kramnick and R. Laurence Moore remind us, ministers sought to repair the godless Constitution by drafting what became known as the Christian Amendment. The Christian Amendment, with ref-

erences to "Almighty God" and to "Lord Jesus Christ," had
the backing of Horace Bushnell, the most influential preacher
of the day. But Lincoln declined to support it. He summed
up his religious sense in his second inaugural. Both warring
halves of the Union, he said, read the same Bible and prayed
to the same God. Each invoked God's aid against each other.
Let us judge not that we be not judged, for "the Almighty has
His own purposes."

Thurlow Weed, the cynical boss of New York, sent Lincoln
a letter of congratulations. "Men are not flattered," Lincoln
replied, "by being shown that there has been a difference of
purpose between the Almighty and them. To deny it, however, in this case is to deny that there is a God governing the
world. It is a truth which I thought needed to be told; and as
whatever of humiliation there is in it falls more directly on
myself, I thought others might afford for me to tell it."

Reinhold Niebuhr was the great American theologian of
the twentieth century. "The combination of moral resolute-
ness about the immediate issues," Niebuhr wrote of Lincoln's
second inaugural, "with a religious awareness of another
dimension of meaning and judgment must be regarded as
almost a perfect model of the difficult but not impossible task
of remaining loyal and responsible toward the moral treasures
of a free civilization while yet having some religious vantage
point over the struggle." Niebuhr added a warning: "As all
God-fearing men of all ages, [we] are never safe against the
temptation of claiming God too simply as the sanctifier of
whatever we most fervently desire."

Is the faith-based presidency good for democracy?

Religion deals in absolutes. Democracy presupposes a plural-istic society that works through negotiation and compromise. John F. Kennedy, the first Roman Catholic president and likely to be the last unless the Vatican behaves itself, said in 1960, "I believe in an America where the separation of church and state is absolute—where no Catholic prelate would tell the President (should he be Catholic) how to act, and no Protestant minister would tell his parishioners for whom to vote—where no church or church school is granted any public funds or political preference."

Is the faith-based presidency even good for religion? Let Andrew Jackson answer that question. In turning down the request by clergy to proclaim a national day of fasting and prayer to stop the cholera epidemic, President Jackson replied that he could not do as the ministers wished "without feel-ing that I might in some degree disturb the security which religion now enjoys in this country in its complete separation from the political concerns of the General Government."

INDEX